# Harry Mathews

## Twayne's United States Authors Series

Frank Day, *Editor*

*Clemson University*

TUSAS 628

HARRY MATHEWS
© *John Foley, Photograph*

# *Harry Mathews*

## Warren Leamon

*Hiroshima University*

Twayne Publishers • New York
Maxwell Macmillan Canada • Toronto
Maxwell Macmillan International • New York  Oxford  Singapore  Sydney

*Harry Mathews*
Warren Leamon

Copyright © by Twayne Publishers
All rights reserved. No part of this book may be reproduced or transmitted in any
form or by any means, electronic or mechanical, including photocopying, recording, or
by any information storage and retrieval system, without permission in writing from
the Publisher.

Twayne Publishers                        Maxwell Macmillan Canada, Inc.
Macmillan Publishing Company             1200 Eglinton Avenue East
866 Third Avenue                         Suite 200
New York, New York 10022                 Don Mills, Ontario M3C 3N1

**Library of Congress Cataloging-in-Publication Data**

Leamon, Warren.
   Harry Mathews / Warren Leamon.
     p.   cm. — (Twayne's United States authors series ; no. 628)
   Includes bibliographical references and index.
   ISBN 0–8057–4008–2 :
   1. Mathews, Harry, 1930–  . —Criticism and interpretation.
   I. Title. II. Series: Twayne's United States authors series ; TUSAS 628
PS3563.A8359Z75  1993
813'.54—dc20                                              93–929
                                                         CIP
The paper used in this publication meets the minimum requirements of American
National Standard for Information Sciences—Permanence of Paper for Printed Library
Materials. ANSI Z3948–1984. ∞

10 9 8 7 6 5 4 3 2 1 (hc)

Printed in the United States of America

*For*
*Professor Nobuyuki Yuasa,*
*who would rather read poetry*

# Contents

# Preface

Harry Mathews is a writer well known in certain literary circles but largely unknown to the general reading public. This is too bad. While it is true that, like the novelists of the modernist tradition of which he sees himself a continuation, he is never content to do one thing at a time, still his fiction, though erudite, is very entertaining—fast paced, witty, humorous—and deserves a much wider audience.

Most reviewers of the early novels, particularly of the first two, emphasized Mathews's playfulness and considered the works for the most part as intellectual games. This is certainly an important dimension in Mathews's writing, but my purpose in this study is to suggest something of the richness of his work, its wonderful multiplicity and ambiguity. Accordingly, I have not attempted to offer "solutions" to the puzzles even when I could come up with them; such puzzle solving is part of the fun for the first-time reader (see my comment later on the plot summaries). I have tried to illustrate how the fiction operates on a number of levels and how those levels relate to one another. In doing this I have emphasized "traditional" or "conventional" elements in the fiction. Many of his admirers may consider such emphasis a distortion. Perhaps they are right. Mathews himself has said that he does not wish to mirror external reality; rather he seeks to draw the reader into the reader's own act of creation. My justification is that I am trying to introduce Mathews to a wider audience than he has heretofore had.

The first chapter is an introduction to Mathews's fiction in which I concentrate on the literary climate in France, where Mathews has spent most of his life since leaving college. But I also try to show that from the beginning Mathews has been a literary maverick and that, in fact, Oscar Wilde may provide as good an insight into his work as Ronald Firbank and Raymond Roussel and other writers usually cited. The second chapter is an interview with Mathews conducted through the mail in 1989. The next four chapters treat the novels in chronological order: *The Conversions* (1962), *Tlooth* (1966), *The Sinking of the Odradek Stadium* (1975), *Cigarettes* (1987). In the final chapter, which considers Mathews's idea of literature as play (or games) in relation to American Realism and the path Realism took with the modernist writers, I discuss the short fiction contained in *Country Cooking and Other Stories* (1980). Doubtless

Mathews's poetry and translations are significant and worthy but they lie outside the scope of this essay.

The chapters on *The Conversions*, *Tlooth*, and *The Sinking of the Odradek Stadium* begin with plot summaries. Of course, these paraphrases can in no way take the place of the novels themselves; they are intended for those who have read the novels but may need to be reminded of their subtle complexities and myriad stories and digressions. (The chapter on *Cigarettes*, because of the nature of the work, is organized somewhat differently.) Those who have read the novels recently or are otherwise familiar with them will want to skip the summaries. I would warn other readers that Mathews's novels, more than those of most writers, contain special and unusual delights for first-time readers, delights that may be spoiled by the summaries.

I wish to thank Harry Mathews for his generosity and cooperation.

# Chronology

| | |
|---|---|
| 1930 | Harry Mathews born 14 February in New York City, the only child of Edward Mathews, architect, and Mary Burchell. |
| 1936–1939 | Educated in private schools in New York City. |
| 1942–1947 | Family moves to Washington, D.C. Mathews attends Groton School. |
| 1947–1948 | Attends Princeton University. |
| 1948–1949 | Serves in Navy. Marries French-born Niki de Saint Phalle in June 1949. |
| 1950 | Transfers to Harvard College. |
| 1951 | Daughter Laura born. |
| 1952 | Graduates from Harvard with a B.A. in music. |
| 1952–1954 | Lives in Paris, Menton, Nice. Studies piano and conducting. Decides to make writing his profession. |
| 1954–1956 | Lives in Deyá, Mallorca. |
| 1955 | Son Philip born. |
| 1956–1960 | Lives in Paris and in Lans-et-Vercors in the French pre-Alps. |
| 1960 | Separates from wife. Moves to Paris, where he lives until 1969. |
| 1962 | *The Conversions.* |
| 1966 | *Tlooth.* |
| 1969–1972 | Lives in Lans. Elected to Oulipo. |
| 1970 | *The Ring: Poems 1956–69.* |
| 1972–1976 | Lives in Paris and Venice. Meets Marie Chaix. |
| 1974 | *The Planisphere.* |
| 1975 | *The Sinking of the Odradek Stadium and Other Novels.* |
| 1976–1986 | Lives in Lans and Paris. Begins spending six months of each year teaching in the United States, first at Bennington College, then at Columbia University. |

1977    *Selected Declarations of Dependence; Trial Impressions.*

1980    *Country Cooking and Other Stories.*

1986    *Le Verger* (in English, *The Orchard*, 1988).

1987    *Cigarettes; Armenian Papers: Poems 1954–1984. Singular Pleasures* in *Grand Street*; published as book in 1988.

1988    *20 Lines a Day; Out of Bounds.*

1989    *The Way Home: Collected Longer Prose.*

1991    *Immeasurable Distances: The Collected Essays; The American Experience.* Awarded a prize for fiction by American Academy for Arts & Letters. DAAD residency in Berlin.

1992    *A Mid-Season Sky: Poems 1954–1991.*

# Chapter One

# Introduction

## The Way Home

Harry Mathews was born into "an upper-middle-class Eastern WASP environment" (his own description), left Princeton after one year, graduated from Harvard with a degree in music, emigrated to Europe (mainly France) where he became the only American member of the Oulipo (an exclusive literary organization in Paris whose members have included Italo Calvino, Raymond Queneau, and Mathews's friend Georges Perec), wrote (among other things) three highly unconventional quest novels and a work celebrating the pleasures and pains of masturbation, and then wrote a novel about the New York worlds of art, finance, and horse racing. Obviously, he defies classification. Or perhaps one must invent a classification that includes him.

The title of his collection of longer prose, *The Way Home* (1989), however, suggests an underlying theme not only of the book but of his life as well. Beginning with one of his most famous works ("Country Cooking"), it moves through a somewhat opaque piece dealing with the imagination ("The Way Home"), then through two experiments ("Their Words, for You" and "Singular Pleasures"), to a memoir of Georges Perec ("The Orchard"). It closes with Mathews's "Autobiography," which, though more a hymn of praise to his teachers, friends and lovers than a penetrating self-portrait, traces his early rebellion against his family and background through his years in Europe to his return (literally and emotionally) to New York. This attempt to escape his background and family, followed by his return to both, are reflected in the book itself in the movement from self-effacing experimental fiction to personal memoir.

A similar development (if it can be called that) can be traced through his four novels. *The Conversions* (1962) and *Tlooth* (1966) achieve detachment through intricate, sometimes fantastic, plots and highly ambiguous narrators. *The Conversions* opens in New York City, but the scene (like Mathews himself) soon moves to Europe, and, with the exception of another section of *The Conversions*, all the action in both novels is set out-

1

side the United States. More than half of *The Sinking of the Odradek Stadium* (1972) is set in the United States, in a Miami of Mathews's own invention. This is an epistolary novel in which the two correspondents emerge from bizarre circumstances as fully realized characters. Finally, in *Cigarettes* (1989), the entire action of which takes place in New York City and upstate New York, characters in a wholly realistic setting come to life through an interweaving of several plots dealing with ordinary middle-class life. While he insists that all fiction is autobiographical in that it comes from the imagination of the author and that "the stories [*Cigarettes*] tells have little enough to do with the events of my life,"[1] the "Autobiography" makes it apparent that *Cigarettes* is the product of family history and personal experience as well.

In "The Way Home" the narrator says, "So much remains to be told, so much remains to be disguised in order to be told" (*Way Home*, 31). One gathers from Mathews's later interviews and essays that there was much disguise in the early fiction, perhaps more than Mathews himself was aware of. Speaking of those novels (mainly, I suppose, *The Conversions* and *Tlooth*), Mathews says, "The earlier works were misread by a great many readers because they always thought I must be doing something else than what was actually there. And so they kept looking past what was right in front of them. One doesn't have to look for symbols, one doesn't have to look for explanations. . . . Many people thought I was being too clever by miles, that I was playing games or just showing off or I don't know what, indulging in a display of erudition."[2] But Mathews insists: "I think [the early books] are very up front. And one way that they're up front is in the terrific unspoken or apparently unspoken drama that goes on in the life of the narrator, one which is barely indicated but always present. . . . In *The Conversions* there's really only one character [the narrator]; the drama you get of one character who can't or doesn't dare tell about himself. I myself find this drama all the more moving by being so painfully, so inadequately expressed" (Tillman, 34).

Mathews—and his friend John Ashbery (Tillman, 34)—may feel great sympathy for the unnamed narrator of *The Conversions*, but as Mathews points out, "The narrator makes only two or three remarks in the course of *The Conversions*—about his wife divorcing him, for instance." And though he adds, "[B]ut they're enough to suggest all the things that he's not saying that he should be saying" (Tillman, 34), how can the reader who knows nothing about Mathews or what he intended feel that sympathy?

Mathews is, in fact, countering what he perceives to be a view of his early fiction with his later theory that it is the reader, not the writer, who is the creator of a literary work (the writer, in rewriting, becomes a reader): "[R]eading is an act of creation for which the writer provides the means" (Tillman, 34). We will take up this theory in the conclusion. For now, it is enough to say that criticisms of his early work[3] seem to present us with something of a false dilemma: one must find in it either pretentious displays or moving emotional experiences. This ignores a vast middle ground that includes the rare delights of erudite novels that are genuinely (as opposed to sophomorically) witty and clever. I don't believe that Mathews was being "too clever" or "showing off" or "indulging in a display," but I think it is fair to say that the appeal of these two novels is mainly intellectual; they derive from and appeal to the human desire for order and meaning, a desire that drives all the arts and sciences. But at practically every turn he thwarts this desire with an insistence upon the actual chaos and confusion of life, its chance and coincidence. This seeming paradox has led some critics to place him among the "postmodernists." Mathews himself says, "[A]side from being confused by the many senses given to 'postmodernism,' I've never used the word to describe anything I've written," and he sees himself as trying "to prolong the modernist tradition."[4]

## Realism and Modernism

The problem is, modernism has accumulated at least as "many senses" as postmodernism. Mathews considers Ronald Firbank to be the father of modernism in that he "transformed the basic narrative procedure of fiction," and he points to Firbank's "dissociation of surface and subject" (Interview). More conventionally, he also calls attention to E. M. Forster's distinction between *story* and *plot* but says, "I don't agree with Forster that plot is what matters, but I'll stick up for storytelling."[5] And elsewhere he says that he prefers "[m]aking a game of inventing the plot" to other "much more dubious points of departure" in fiction than, "[r]epresentation ('realism') and 'self expression'" (Interview).

Although it is not his intention, what Mathews calls attention to is the confusion that lay at the heart of modernism from the very beginning when writers attempted to embrace the relativism that came to dominate Western culture around the turn of the century without aban-

doning Realism with its insistence on a belief in a meaning, a significance, outside the work itself. The mainstream of modernist fiction
embodied the old principle of metaphor: story becomes plot when surface depends for its meaning on something beyond the surface. Thus fiction can find fulfillment only outside the fiction. Writers are judged by
the appropriateness of their work, how it can be interpreted in the light
of current "reality." In the modernist period, for example, the sterility of
contemporary society was accepted as reality by both the intellectual
establishment created by the Eliot/Pound circle and the Marxist critics,
and works were invariably interpreted in relation to such sterility: *The
Waste Land* (Western decadence), *The Sound and the Fury* (Southern
degeneration), *The Day of the Locust* (American vulgarity and hopeless-
ness), *Parade's End* and *Nightwood* (traditional values in the rising tide of
nihilism), etc.

The writers of these works clung to the idea of the artist as one who
embodies transcendent meaning in an artifact. Applied to fiction, this
meant that shifting and conflicting points of view reflect the everyday
reality of a world seeking meaning. Unity was the highest aesthetic principle, and metaphor and paradox, because they seemed capable of unifying opposites, became the dominant aesthetic devices.[6] What was
new—or at least quite different—was the way in which writers, strug-
gling with the realities of relativism and trying to find a substitute for
"self expression," began to create narratives in which action dissolves into
various perspectives as differing points of view revolve around a center.
Looking back, we can see that the writers couldn't escape self-expression;
they could only fashion masks to conceal it. But the desire for detachment
led to a new kind of fiction. No longer did the reader interpret character
and action in light of a central significance; now the reader searched character and action for clues to the nature of significance itself.

E. M. Forster summed up the situation in 1927 when he distin-
guished between *story* and *plot* and asserted that plot lies at the very
heart of fiction. Story involves only "and then" and can be told by cave
men sitting around a fire. Plot involves "why," in so doing introduces
cause and effect, and is capable of the highest aesthetic development.[7]
The purpose of plot is not only to unify the work and add mystery; plot
also assures the reader that life itself has an order, a pattern. The importance of fiction lies in its imitation of the order that exists in life.

Forster's book, along with Percy Lubbock's *The Craft of Fiction* (both
spinoffs of Henry James's ideas), was to be enormously influential in the
interpretation of modernist fiction. In particular, all three writers seemed

to insist that plot is what binds the aesthetic to the moral in fiction. But five years before Forster's *Aspects of the Novel* was written, James Joyce had finished *Ulysses*, in which he brought Realism to its highest pitch in the first 10 episodes. Then, with the Sirens episode, the work takes a turn that has been controversial to the present day.[8] Abandoning the cause-and-effect development of Realism, he immerses the reader in the present moment. Expanding minutes, contracting eons, the novel pulsates with an immediacy never before (or since) accomplished in fiction. Whether or not that immediacy collapses into the incoherence of lived existence, Joyce developed to its fullest extent the principle so many artists and critics have espoused: fiction should make the reader experience life. But in achieving immediacy, Joyce sacrificed plot. Though *Ulysses* is filled with wonderful stories and with ingenious inventions that may or may not hold the work together, it certainly does not move according to the old literary laws of Realism. In fact, in attempting to turn literature into life, Joyce managed to increase the reader's awareness of *Ulysses* as fiction.

## Rediscovery of Raymond Roussel

*Ulysses* (1922) and *Aspects of the Novel* (1927) can be taken to represent the two poles of literary modernism as regards plot. Between these two poles lies Mathews's view: plot as a game. Each of his first three novels makes use of a narrative somewhat similar to plot in that it establishes a chain of cause and effect that runs through the novel from beginning to end. But in each instance the plot is also a puzzle to be solved by the reader. And at almost every turn the plot is stymied by storytelling, by one outrageous appeal to curiosity after another. And none of the plots has an ending (this is not to say that the novels themselves do not have endings). Moreover, the lack of a conventional ending in each instance is related to the point of view, the narrative voice (or voices in *Odradek*). What Mathews writes, as we will see, are three novels that on one level simply stop (or rather, like life itself, come to no conclusion), while on another level they provide material for any number of "endings."

Mathews's works do possess unity, but they do not achieve it through the old principle of metaphor; and, following his reading of Firbank, he uses points of view that go further than mainstream modernism did in the "dissociation of subject and surface." Why did Mathews, who seems to have been so attracted to the modernist period, feel the need to experiment with it? What seems to be the answer comes in an interview in which Mathews says that his early attempts at fiction were unsuccessful because "I'd always thought that to write fiction you had to write more or less autobiographical stories, or stories of things that you'd observed in the world. It's terribly hard to do that; at least it was terribly hard for me—to make it sing and glow."[9] Mathews felt the need of the constraints of poetry, its "arbitrary, illogical" demands. It was in the work of Raymond Roussel, largely forgotten since his death in 1933 until he was rediscovered by the French New Novelists, that Mathews says he found the solution to his problem: "Roussel showed how this can be done in prose and so for me opened up the whole possibility of writing fiction" (Ashbery, 41).

Mathews discovered Roussel's fiction after he went to France in the early 1950s. At that time the literary scene was dominated by Alain Robbe-Grillet and the New Novelists, who were in revolt against modernism. Attacking what they considered bourgeois conceptions of character and plot and advocating "presence" and "the present" in fiction, the New Novelists sought to fashion self-contained works that broke the conventional metaphorical connection between language and ideology.

The theory of the New Novel is now a part of standard literary criticism, and all of Robbe-Grillet's assertions have been convincingly challenged. But what was crucial about the movement as regards Mathews was the shift from ritual to play (games) that characterized theory and practice. Believing that modernism was essentially a ritual used by writers to involve the reader in a reality (or illusion) beyond the text, the New Novelists sought to produce works of art that were self-contained in the sense that they did not depend on something outside themselves for unity (and therefore meaning). Their answer was games, which by their nature contain rules and a beginning, middle, and end. And so it is not surprising that Robbe-Grillet and others not only became interested in detective stories (in both literature and film) but also turned back to the work of Roussel.

At first glance a novel by Roussel seems very much in the tradition of surrealism: a rammer suspended from a blimp creating a mosaic of discolored teeth, a diamond that makes music, a hairless cat and Danton's brain suspended in a water-filled glass tank (the cat can make the brain speak), performing sea horses, etc. And he was very much admired by the surrealists until it began to become apparent that, far from working out of the unconscious or subconscious by free association, Roussel had fashioned his grotesque artificial world from certain rigidly adhered-to formulas: semantic and phonic word pairings, patterns set up by lines of poetry perhaps chosen at random (usually from Hugo but from others, including poems for children), puns (sometimes related to word pairings, sometimes not). Writing at the end of his life, he provided keys to some of the scenes and stories in his work that indicated an obsession with constraints, an aesthetic impulse infused with masochism.[10]

Robbe-Grillet asserts that Roussel's work "has exercised its spell over several generations of writers" and he must be counted "among the direct ancestors of the modern novel."[11] In accounting for Roussel's importance, he first points out that in Roussel's work, "since there is never anything beyond the thing described . . . no supernature . . . no symbolism . . . the eye is forced to rest on the very surface of things." On the other hand, "mystery is one of the formal themes most readily used by Roussel." But Roussel's mysteries "are enigmas set forth too clearly, analyzed too objectively, and too evidently asserted as enigmas. . . . After the rebus comes the explanation, and everything is back where it belongs." Roussel uses mystery to engage the reader, but, "once again, a signification that is too transparent coincides with total opacity" (Robbe-Grillet, 81–82).

But Roussel's work does have unity and therefore meaning: "The narrative has effected, before our eyes . . . a profound change in what the world—and language—means." And "another striking characteristic of these images . . . [is] *instantaneity* . . . everything is given as in movement, but frozen in the middle of that movement, immobilized by the representation which leaves all gestures, falls, conclusions, etc., eternalizing them in the imminence of their end and severing them from their meaning" (Robbe-Grillet, 85).

According to Robbe-Grillet, Roussel is an existentialist in whose writing words (and the things they represent) are severed from their traditional meaning, the old capitalist/Christian signification with which earlier writers "trapped" the reader. What emerges from his work is "a universe of fixity, of repetition, of absolute obviousness." And Robbe-Grillet admits: "[T]he trap reappears, but it is of another nature. Obviousness, transparency preclude the existence of *higher worlds*, of any transcendence. . . . [F]rom this world before us we discover we can no longer escape" (Robbe-Grillet, 87). And, obviously, Robbe-Grillet hasn't escaped metaphor. Instead he has substituted one metaphor for another: nature as always leading to something else is rejected for nature as frozen in a world in which always "the foam of the motionless wave is about to fall back" (Robbe-Grillet, 87).

Robbe-Grillet's interpretation of Roussel is not the only one,[12] and Mathews seems not to have been familiar with it before he wrote *The Conversions* (and possibly *Tlooth*). But the discovery of Roussel that pervaded the literary atmosphere was no less important to Mathews than it was to Robbe-Grillet and the New Novelists. Moreover, Robbe-Grillet isolates and emphasizes the problems of time and space as they appear in modern fiction, and Mathews acknowledges what Robbe-Grillet acknowledges: "There is no ending, no final form in nature" (Ash, 26). There is certainly nothing new or surprising in this observation, and its implication for the novel is obvious: plot makes storytelling unrealistic; each individual's life is full of endings, but in fact it has only one real ending, and even that one, seen from another perspective, is not an ending. This is not a problem in the spatial arts or in music; and it is not much of a problem in poetry because of the poet's use of arbitrary devices; and in fiction, up until recently, it wasn't perceived as a problem.

## The Importance of Storytelling

Mathews's first three novels are not realistic in their fidelity to mundane reality. Nor is their central theme the individual in conflict with a corrupt and tyrannical society. And though it has been observed that fantasy is realistic in that it always exists as a comment on the real, Mathews doesn't seem particularly interested in satire. A Soviet prison camp, Southeast Asia, Miami are settings fraught with the possibilities for criticisms of or attacks on society (especially when one considers the time, the 1960s and 1970s), but Mathews seems to choose such settings in order *not* to moralize; in that sense they call attention to the apolitical nature of his work, which does not mean that Mathews is apolitical.

Yet in a curious and very elusive way these novels do retain a connection with mundane reality. Mathews gives us characters with enough roundness and vitality to make us at least wonder why, in the case of the first two novels, they are not more fully developed. And in *The Sinking of the Odradek Stadium* characterization becomes as important as storytelling and invention. On the other hand, one can see why Mathews says that he is working in the modernist tradition: *The Conversions*, with its underpinning of myth borrowed in part from Robert Graves's *The White Goddess*, owes much to Joyce and Eliot as well as to Roussel or Queneau (though both the French writers make use of myth themselves). If one were to look back at the first three novels from the perspective of the fourth, *Cigarettes*, one might discern a movement toward older concepts of Realism. Such would be appropriate in an author who delights in turning things upside down, in inventing things that don't work or that accomplish the opposite of what they were designed to do.

I think that it is this remnant of Realism that has kept Mathews from becoming more popular. He is neither mainstream modernist nor pure experimenter. Rather he has been influenced by both, and his own work shows those influences in the middle ground it takes between invention and metaphor. He accomplishes what the New Novelists wanted to accomplish, the breaking down of the entrenched connection between surface reality and traditional notions of transcendence, but he retains the old sense of the importance of emotion, of feeling—tenuously in the first two novels, more fully in the next two—mainly because he doesn't attempt to deny the temporal aspect of fiction, that it must exist in time, and because, no matter the extent to which fiction is a game, neither reader nor writer can escape the mimetic quality of language.

John Ash cites Brigid Brophy's contention that "narrative is a drug" that if the nineteenth created "vast readership for long novels loaded down with realistic lumber. This is a problem for contemporary novelists. The reader gets carried uncritically along because he simply wants to know what happens next." He then asks Mathews, "How do you distinguish literature from pulp fiction without frustrating the reader's expectations?" Mathews replies:

> For me the problem has been: how do you do without narrative in an extended work? Quite a number of people have tried to do without it— good writers writing interesting, witty sentences and giving up narrative as good modernists should, and my attention lapses after a mere five or ten sentences. Narrative clearly is a drug but let's hope it can be used intelligently. . . . [P]erhaps what makes narrative so compulsive is the fact that there *is* an ending. There is no ending, no final form in nature. When I started writing I felt my only talent was for narrative. It was something I didn't have to do too much about since it would just come out anyway, and, of course, it's thoroughly stymied in book after book. The main narrative is always very simple—solving a riddle, seeking revenge, finding a treasure—and it gets utterly obliterated by interruptions and digressions. (Ash, 26)

This passage is an excellent introduction to Mathews's fictional technique. Though he never abandons his gift for storytelling, he resists the shaping of narrative into plot in the old modernist sense. Instead he seems to be content with a main narrative that carries the reader through numerous attempts to frustrate it. This simple story keeps the reader oriented through "interruptions and digressions." This suggests what Mathews states elsewhere (Interview), that the word games, the codes, the hidden imitations and allusions, the mathematical equations in his work were essential to him in the composition of his novels but not essential to the reader's understanding of them.

What Mathews has to say about his discovery of Roussel has other implications as well. The postmodernist critique of Realism (and the modernist version of it), from the New Novelists to the deconstructionists and the exponents of metafiction, is built, in part at least, upon paranoia: Realism is often seen as a product of a conspiracy to make Realism synonymous with the novel and a part of a political battle.[13] Going along with this paranoia is the underlying assumption that Realism makes art inferior to life rather than merely separate from it. Once this idea is rejected and life is no longer seen as superior to art, then the postmodern literary chain is complete: nature supplies the raw material for art and art supplies the raw material for the highest of all literary forms, criticism. Within this system validity is substituted for truth, and the interpreter dominates and controls the creator. Mathews is wonderfully free of this struggle for power. This is one of the reasons that his works seem to many critics more entertaining than those of other experimenters.

## The Ambiguity of Masks: Wilde's Fable

The other reason lies in his refusal either to ignore or to condescend to the reader. As we will see, this concern for the reader prevents Mathews not only from abandoning his gift for storytelling but also from falling into a feigned concern for the reader that characterizes much metafiction. Mathews says that his "only talent was for narrative" and that "it's thoroughly stymied in book after book." And while it's true—as the interviewer, Ash, points out—that the main idea is not completely destroyed, that Mathews "can do very complex things and the reader can still hang on to that original idea. . . . [I]t carries you through [the book]" (Ash, 26–27), the question remains: why "stymie" the "talent . . . for narrative?" An answer would seem to lie in the life and work of a writer who may be as important as either Firbank or Roussel to an understanding of Mathews's fiction. Mathews quotes that writer at the beginning of *Cigarettes*:

"Let me tell you a story on the subject," said the Linnet.

"Is the story about me?" asked the Water-rat. "If so, I will listen to it, for I am extremely fond of fiction."[14]

Oscar Wilde's words forewarn the reader: although Mathews's novel may be, in part at least, drawn from his own life and background, it is nonetheless a fiction. But the warning, for one who knows the work of Wilde (and Mathews), is a bit more complex.

In Wilde's "The Devoted Friend" Hans considers Hugh the Miller to be his best friend when in fact the Miller uses and abuses little Hans while proclaiming how devoted he is to him: "Indeed, so devoted was the rich Miller to little Hans, that he would never go by his garden without leaning over the wall and plucking a large nosegay, or a handful of sweet herbs, or filling his pockets with plums and cherries if it was the fruit season . . . [but] the rich Miller never gave little Hans anything in return" (Wilde, 679–80). Accordingly, during the hard winter the Miller will not invite his devoted friend to dinner because, he says, that will cause little Hans to envy him, and envy is a sin. He promises to give little Hans an old broken wheelbarrow (which he never does) and uses the promise to justify further mistreatment of him. All the while little Hans praises the Miller for his noble sentiments and fine talk. Finally, the Miller, without realizing it, causes the death of little Hans and at the funeral proclaims that he was his best friend: "I had given him my wheelbarrow, and now I don't know what to do with it. . . . I will certainly take care not to give away anything again. One always suffers for being generous" (Wilde, 692).

The story contains a "truth"—there are people like the Miller who are totally and unconsciously selfish and self-serving—and the opposite "truth"—there are people like little Hans who are totally and unconsciously unselfish and generous. Both characters are "devoted"—the Miller to himself, little Hans to the Miller—and the title is both literal and ironic. At the end the Water-rat wants to know "what became of the Miller," and when the Linnet says that he doesn't know and he doesn't care, the Water-rat accuses him of having "no sympathy in your nature." The Water-rat obviously thinks that the Miller (the character most like himself) is the hero, which leads the Linnet to remark, "I'm afraid you don't quite see the moral of the story." The Water-rat is outraged to discover that the story has a moral. "I think you should have told me that before you began. If you had done so, I certainly would not have listened to you" (Wilde, 692–93).

But what is the moral? That one should not be blindly selfish? Or its opposite, that one should not be blindly unselfish? The answer would seem to be both. The Linnet thinks the former applicable to the Water-rat, but the reader is far more likely, before considering the story carefully, to think the latter the point of the parable.

By now "The Devoted Friend" is a children's story, a cynical tale, a cautionary tale, a parable, a "decadent" joke (the Miller and little Hans come together in a sado-masochistic relationship that gives pleasure to them both), or perhaps anything else that the reader might make of it. The Duck, who has not heard the story, paddles up to the Linnet after the Water-rat has gone back in his hole and says that she feels sorry for him because "I have a mother's feelings, and I can never look at a confirmed bachelor without tears coming into my eyes." This observation would seem to be totally irrelevant to any meaning that the story might have—if the story has a meaning. Or maybe the point is that confirmed bachelors are to be pitied and not scorned for their selfishness. At least, that is what the Duck would have gotten from the story because that is what she would have brought to it.

And at the end the story takes yet another turn. "I told [the Water-rat] a story with a moral," the Linnet says. The Duck replies, "Ah, that is always a very dangerous thing to do." And suddenly, in the very last sentence of the story, the narrator speaks in the first person for the first time: "And I quite agree with her." Why is a moral dangerous? Because it can change your life? Because it might cause the Water-rat to see himself as he really is and consequently make him more like little Hans, who is destroyed by his devotion to friendship? Art and life, the aesthetic and the moral, should never mix. The narrator seems to agree with the critic and, therefore, with the Water-rat. Unless he is being ironic.

Whatever the narrator is being, his is simply another opinion. For at the end Wilde's entering the story himself reminds us that there are no "omniscient" narrators, that omniscience is a game played between reader and writer, one of countless possible games, another being that Oscar Wilde is the narrator. But which Oscar Wilde? The mask or the reality behind the mask?

I have devoted what might seem an inordinate amount of space to Wilde's story because it provides insight not only into *Cigarettes* but also into all Mathews's novels. They are all, in one way or another, about stories, the effects of stories on stories, and the relation of stories to life and love and passion. And reading Mathews, one is constantly reminded of Wilde's belief that "a truth in art is that whose contradictory is also true."[15]  Like Wilde, Mathews is richly ambiguous about the relationship between life and art, between the moral and the aesthetic. Consequently, both authors constantly undercut seemingly obvious judgments (as in "The Devoted Friend"). The existence of a spiritual dimension is never denied, but it always hovers on the periphery of the game the authors have designed. And in entering the game with the author, the reader puts his own moral and spiritual beliefs into play.

A major difference would seem to be that Wilde almost never uses a first person point of view,[16] while Mathews seldom uses anything else. But even here the difference may be more apparent than real. Wilde believed that when a man speaks about himself in his own voice, he lies; only when he assumes a mask does he tell the truth about himself. And the relationship between the real-life Wilde and the Wilde who narrates the fiction is still—and probably always will be—the subject of much debate. Mathews, in his novels, writes as a "dilettantish mulatto," a musician/dentist, an Indochinese woman, a Miami librarian, a masochistic homosexual. And while we are tempted to think that, because he is an "upper-middle-class Eastern WASP," he is being most autobiographical in *Cigarettes*, we should keep in mind what Wilde said and consider that the narrators in the first two novels, written while Mathews was an expatriate living in Europe, are deracinated wanderers (most likely Americans). *Cigarettes*, written after his "return" to America, explores his own class and background but does so from the point of view of an outcast, a pariah. Again and again Mathews assumes the mask of the searcher, the person on a quest that as we will see, can be interpreted on several levels.

# Chapter Two

# Harry Mathews: An Interview

*Welch D. Everman says of your novels, "In the end, the words are simply there on the page, pointing to nothing beyond themselves." And Eric Mottram says, "Mathews invents plots as games." Yet in a recent interview you agreed with Lynne Tillman's observation: "{F}aith in language, as a way to communicate, is like faith in religion . . . you have to believe in language, you have faith that you can communicate, even if you're not really able to communicate, as you have in a religion" {Tillman, 35}. Are Everman and Mottram right? If they are, then how do you reconcile their positions with yours?*

Your question baffles me, although not for the reasons you may think. To address Mottram's remark first: what is there to be reconciled between the idea of games and that of communication? Aside possibly from solitaire, in what game does communication not take place, all the time and often at a high pitch of intensity? For obvious, highly paid examples, watch Lendl and Becker face to face, and watch the people watching them. Perec gives a perhaps less familiar example in his description, in the opening pages of *Life A User's Manual*, of the relation between the puzzle creator and the puzzle solver. Playing games does not replace communication in the use of language; it gives a direct access to it. Mottram quite properly refers to game playing when talking about my plots, a domain in which it's particularly appropriate, since the plot has an inevitably "abstract" element in it that must be attended to independently of everything else (even, at the limit, of subject)—its workability, its process of starting some place and getting some place else. Making a game of inventing the plot means both recognizing its abstractness for what it is and affording oneself new, unpredictable positions from which to approach one's material (by which I mean everything else). Representation ("realism") and "self expression" strike me as much more dubious points of departure.

As for Everman's statement, I don't remember its context, but on seeing it here, two thoughts come to mind about its applicability to what I write. First, I'd be happy to think that my written language somehow visibly disclaims any justification by subject or external reference: all values of thought, feeling, and imagination are created entirely by the reader using the materials I supply on the page. Second, I certainly intend to make it as difficult as possible for any reader not to realize that the experience he is having is that of reading (rather than an experience of what the written words are describing or representing); this seems a useful thing to do, since it corresponds to what is in fact happening and constitutes a truly realistic element in what I write. I don't consider reading a substitute for other kinds of experience but as one form of experience among many, one that is rather more productive than many others. Again, I can't see why making a theater of the act of reading in any way precludes or limits communication. It's the particular domain where literary communication takes place, just as tennis is the domain (when they're on the court) for communication between Lendl and Becker. I don't think much in the way of passion, self-expression, human drama, or even political rhetoric (I was thinking of tennis!) gets left out.

*Everman's criticism is echoed by critics who find a lack of compassion in your early novels. How do you respond to such criticism?*

Everman's remark was not intended as criticism in the sense of reproach, although from another hand it might well have been. As for the lack of compassion . . . (A parenthesis first: Richard III, Smerdiakov, and J. R. demonstrate their author's compassion more than Ophelia, Raskolnikov, and J. R.'s "kind" and unmemorable brother. Certainly they prove the authors' compassion for the audience: these are the characters people thrill to.) The sense of a lack of compassion in *The Conversions* and *Tlooth* is I think the result of looking *past* what is written rather than simply reading it. The sentences in the two books may be stony in tone but are "actually" (i.e., physically) tense and intense (I guess it would be more accurate to say the sequences of sentences; I don't mean each sentence by itself). I think an attentive reader, experiencing the succession of sentences and chapters, confronted by the combination of an unnaturally, almost inhumanly inexpressive tone with a profusion of strange and often painful events, will inevitably start asking why this is so—ultimately, why are the narrators so obsessively denying themselves the right to express their feelings?  As I think I mentioned in another interview [Tillman, 34], John Ashbery was one reader who immediately spotted the rare moments in *The Conversions* where the narrator speaks of his personal life as crucial to the sense of the book. The first two novels have only one character, the narrators, both of them distraught with their obsessions. They are the sole objects of compassion. But where must that compassion come from?

*The previous question raises a central point in criticism of postmodernist works: To what extent does the postmodernist theory of character—its attack on the traditional (i.e., "realistic") concept of character—make compassion impossible?*

"Postmodernist works:" aside from being confused by the many senses given to "postmodernism," I've never used the word to describe anything I've written, and my ambition has been to prolong the modernist tradition, which for me represents the resumption of an endless and never-to-be-concluded battle against the legion of answer-gatherers. This is *not* in any way directed towards you: I'm delighted to supply answers to your questions, and another set to the same questions tomorrow.

Modernism brought to the writing of fiction, which as you know began as a "sentimental" diversion, concerns that preceded it and that had been left aside or masked in the nineteenth century. Compassion and other respectable feelings aren't a necessary ingredient in modernist works, but I assert that they are in no way incompatible with them. (Sometimes compassion is both powerfully present *and* irrelevant.) Kafka's compassion strikes me as no less intense than Dostoyevski's.

*In a conversation with John Ash {Ash, 21} you mention Joyce as important to modernism, but you say that you think Firbank is the father of modernism. So: What in the writing of Joyce most influenced the development of modernism and could you expand a bit on your admiration for Firbank?*

(Another parenthesis: while looking for the remark about Joyce, I came on these lines of J. Ash's: "It seems to me that what is fashionably termed 'metafiction'—the self-reflexive fiction that always reminds you of its fictiveness—which you say readers often find irritating or difficult, is in some ways a more generous, less authoritarian kind of writing since it seeks to involve the reader; it always thinks of the reader and doesn't try to swamp him or her with a narrative that imitates life" [Ash, 26]. This seems succinctly relevant to your earlier questions.)

What I said was: "Of course Firbank was the great formal innovator. He invented modernism, more so than Joyce really." The "really" acknowledges the fact that Joyce was a prodigious formal innovator. To my mind Firbank's superiority resides in this: Joyce's innovations have affected us mainly in the domain of style and the way his material is presented, whereas Firbank transformed the basic narrative procedure of fiction. This is a hastily concocted remark; I wouldn't find it interesting to get stuck in an argument defending it.

Aside from his abundant surface delights, and they're rich indeed, Firbank has a formal originality that Evelyn Waugh described in an interesting if rather condescending essay published during the twenties[1]: essentially, his dissociation of surface and subject, a dissociation overt and conspicuous. The tragedies underlying his works are never laid bare, we only glimpse them from a distance through the casual and often hilarious events recounted to us. From this distancing the tragedies only gain in power, and in their power to move us. This manner of storytelling perfectly enacts Firbank's great compassion (to resume our original topic)—it's a genuinely modernist approach to that question.

*You arrived in France at about the time that the New Novel was all the rage and Robbe-Grillet, Sarraute, Pinget, and others were doing battle with the establishment. Did these aesthetic battles influence you in the writing of* The Conversions *and* Tlooth?

When I wrote *The Conversions* [1959], I'd never heard of the New Novel. I may have read some Butor and Robbe-Grillet before starting *Tlooth*, but although I liked them well enough, I wasn't interested by what they were doing, and I think I can honestly say they never influenced me at all.

*Regarding* The Conversions, *would you say that everything in the novel—everything the narrator sees, hears, and experiences in his quest—is relevant to that quest?*

Yes and no. The narrator seems to be a plaything in some scheme of Grent Wayl's invention, but we can hardly assume that Mr. Wayl is sure of getting the results he wanted; would the narrator have obtained the fortune even if he'd found the answer to the third riddle? (After all, you probably have found the answer, and what good did it do you?) The implication is that the narrator, Mr. Wayl, and everything else is the victim or perhaps the subject of yet another design; and it's to this design that everything the narrator sees, hears, and experiences is relevant. (*Much* of it is relevant to the quest as well.)

*A number of critics have asserted that* The Sinking of the Odradek Stadium *is "Nabokovian." What do you think they mean? Do you agree?*

I don't know why *Odradek* is thought to be Nabokovian—perhaps because of the way it "burns itself out"? I've read Nabokov with pleasure, but I haven't reflected much on the nature of that pleasure.

*Did you have any association with the Oulipo before you formally became a member of the group in 1972?*

Like most members of the Oulipo other than its founders, I was a guest of honor at one of its meetings shortly before my election to the group. My friendship with Perec aside, I had no other association with it. (I first heard of it in 1968.)

*Keith Cohen says, "Harry Mathews's work is always based on a hidden pattern,"[2] and he goes on to apply this observation to some of your short stories. Is what Cohen says true of your novels? If so, why should the patterns be "hidden?" Finally, you wouldn't want to provide a "key" for us, would you?*

I have to say first of all that Keith Cohen, whose intelligence and whose brilliance as a fiction writer I admire hugely, is famously wrong in his specific applications of the idea of a "hidden pattern." The idea itself is not wrong, but it should be clarified. In some cases there is a "real" hidden pattern, that is, one worth looking for: for example, in "Country Cooking" there is a second subject, repeatedly referred to but never stated, underlying the presentation of the recipe. It is hidden because of the nature of the subject and because the "effect" of the subject is experienced (probably?) by the reader without explicit presentation. In other cases the hidden pattern is no more than the structure or procedure that enabled me to organize the work. Once the work is written, the pattern becomes irrelevant and of no use in reading the work (no more than knowing the solution to the third enigma in *The Conversions*): it is in no sense the point of the work. I couldn't give you these constructive patterns if I wanted to because as soon as I'm through with them I throw them away. The fact that a work is written according to such a pattern does matter insofar as it makes the reader aware that something else is going on (or has gone on)—he becomes exceptionally curious and alert. At least that's *my* experience as a reader. Raymond Queneau goes into this question at some length in one of his essays (or perhaps interviews). Perhaps I should add that in the Oulipo there are two factions: one that advocates publishing or announcing one's formal constraint, the other that advocates concealing it. Perec belonged to the first faction, Queneau to the second.

*To what extent are your novels autobiographical? That is, do you make use of your own experiences, things that happened to you, to people you know, etc.? Is* Cigarettes *more autobiographical than your previous works?*

I presume all my novels to be autobiographical. In *Cigarettes* I made use of a great many "objective" experiences: while none of the characters is modeled on (or indeed resembles) anyone I've known, I did work as a hotwalker at a race track, my first wife had a nasty time with hyperthyroidism, I've had gallery owners as friends, etc. In the earlier novels, almost everything of this kind is invented; the "autobiographical" element, if it is present, has nothing to do with "objective" experience but is the result of my success in trying to outwit my censorious conscious mind by giving myself all those uncompassionate games to play: their purpose was to let the unconscious manifest itself on the page. (Example: *The Conversions* as an exploration of the castration complex?) *Cigarettes* in its characters, events, and plot is no more autobiographical than the other novels: "everything must come from the imagination."

*Most critics find* Cigarettes *very different from your previous novels, and you yourself have commented on some of the differences. Would you go so far as to say that* Cigarettes *maintains some of the superficial aspects of postmodernism but abandons the principles of the movement? That is, does* Cigarettes *abide by the letter but not spirit of postmodernism?*

*Cigarettes* (since you ask me) abandons the superficial aspects of modernism and maintains its principles. It abides by the spirit but not the letter of modernism.

*Of late, Georges Perec is getting much more attention than he has had heretofore in the U.S. Why do you think this is so? I mean, aside from the fact that his writing deserves attention, is there anything going on right now in our culture that would increase his popularity?*

Georges Perec has been getting more attention of late in the U.S. because he has at last been published here: there is no earlier time to compare this one to. The publication of *Life A User's Manual* in France similarly transformed his reputation, which had waned considerably since the original success of *Les Choses*.

*Finally, a large question that overlaps with questions I've already asked: In your interview with Tillman you say, "The earlier works were misread by a great many readers because they always thought I must be doing something else than what was actually there. . . . Many people thought . . . I was playing games . . . indulging in a display of erudition" {Tillman, 34}. Yet shortly thereafter, when you begin to talk about* Cigarettes, *you say, "I promised myself not to do any-*

*thing I'd already done in my earlier books. No erudition, no language games."*
*Do you contradict yourself and aren't there some "games" in* Cigarettes?

There is no contradiction: playing games was *part* of what I did. I played
the biggest game of all in constructing *Cigarettes*. The games I didn't
play in *Cigarettes* were (as I said in the [Tillman] interview) the *language*
games.

The point of the elaborate erudite constructions and of all the language games (except for Twang's use of Panamese) was that they signified nothing: not that they were pointless, but that they demonstrated
pointlessness. Felix Namque would have painted the same paintings
without his machine; the Nestorian interpretation of the *res* paper turned
into hot air. The schoolboy arag-language of the Voe-Doge brothers was
used by them for absolutely circular noncommunication; the readership
of the *Pape Niger* text can hardly be imagined outside the readers of
*Tlooth*; Zachary's contamination by the jargon of the big con is evidence
of his psychic deterioration and isolation. And Twang demonstrates the
same principle through its reverse: she emerges as a smart, lively woman
as she emerges from the tangles (in English) of her native tongue.

In *Cigarettes* there is only one "game," which is its plot—no, not even
that: the way I made my way to the plot. (The distinction is worth making because the plot has its own structure, one I find interesting and
indeed essential; but that structure isn't any kind of game.) In the earlier books there were similar games, as well as obvious language games,
among many other forms of poetic activity: and all these activities were
means to express my passionately held idea of the truth.

# Chapter Three

# Too Many Clues: *The Conversions*

## The Quest: The First Question

"When was a stone not a king?"

*The Conversions* opens abruptly in the house of "the wealthy amateur Grent Wayl" to which the narrator (who will never be named) has been invited for "an evening's diversion."[1] During the party Wayl takes the narrator upstairs, shows him a ritual adze, and asks him to "interpret" the "wiry engravings, depicting seven scenes." The narrator attempts an interpretation which does not satisfy Wayl. They return to the party where the narrator and Beatrice and Isidore Fod (Wayl's niece and nephew) participate in a worm race; that is, each is assigned a worm ("dried out but alive; moisture will quicken them") and must perform musically as the worm progresses. "The race will end with the first high *do*," and as a prize the winner will receive the adze. The narrator's worm wins the race and he receives the prize.

Curious about the circumstances of the party and the race, the narrator decides to pursue the mystery of the engravings on the adze. He calls Miss Dryrein, Wayl's secretary, for information. She says that she knows nothing and suggests he "consult the former owner of the adze, from whom it had been bought only a few months before." The narrator meets with this person, "a minor novelist," and finds out that he won it also, as prize in a word game played with gypsies on the Long Island waterfront. "The chief [of the gypsies] explained that the pictures engraved on its head portrayed the life of some ancient wonderqueen of theirs, from her birth to her burning. Then he and several other men discussed the last scene shown on it—the one with moon, arrows, and fish—which they couldn't understand, still less agree on" (*Conversions*, 34–35).

The next morning the narrator is awakened by Beatrice Fod, who attempts to buy the adze from him for a "price close to a million dollars." As she leaves, her brother Isidore arrives and tries to buy the adze. The narrator then learns why they have come: Mr. Wayl has died and practically all of his vast estate (more than $300 million) is left to

> . . . such person as has in his possession a golden adze hereunder described and who is able to provide a satisfactory explanation of its meaning, purport, uses and significance, now and at all times, the said explanation to be verified by my executrix or by such executors as she may appoint according to the answers given by any qualifying person to the following three questions:
> 1) When was a stone not a king?
> 2) What was *La Messe de Sire Fadevant?*
> 3) Who shaved the Old Man's Beard? (*Conversions*, 46)

During the funeral procession, "at the corner of Park Avenue and Forty-ninth Street . . . the coffin exploded. . . . [T]he panic . . . led to one death and many injuries. . . . Investigators concluded . . . that Mr. Wayl's watch [the will had stipulated that it be placed in the coffin with him] had triggered the tragic detonation" (*Conversions*, 47).

The narrator begins his quest for answers to the three questions by visiting Wayl's surviving relatives. He goes first to the Fods, neither of whom is able to tell him anything about the adze. He next visits Allen (Al) Cavallo in the Astoria Agrarians' Hospital and finds him "an inhuman and pitiful sight . . . insane and in unremitting pain" (*Conversions*, 58) and so, like the Fods, able to tell him nothing.

At this point the narrator discovers that the adze was shipped to America from Alloa, in Scotland, and he decides to go there. On the way he visits Wayl's remaining relatives. In Paris he calls "on M. Purkinje, a distant cousin of Mr. Wayl's on his mother's side," who because of his participation in the Panarchist Uprising of 1911 "had passed most of his life in the political wing of Les Innocents, France's largest prison" (*Conversions*, 59). Purkinje and two other men sit "motionless, only sipping their wine from time to time. . . . I was obliged, empty-handed again, to leave Mr. Wayl's cousin" (*Conversions*, 63–64).

Next the narrator visits the Voe-Doge brothers in Chelsea, whom he finds "engaged in furious argument" in an utterly incomprehensible language. Realizing he would understand nothing they might tell him, the narrator gives up, but as he is leaving he notices a painting, initialed F. N. It is "identical with the third scene of the adze—the supposed sanctification of the saint by Jesus. To my surprise, the brass plate on the bottom of its frame read: *The Crowning of the King"* (*Conversions*, 65).

The next five chapters (*Conversions*, 66–105) take place in Scotland at The Customs House of Alva. The narrator hears music as he approaches ("partsong written in antique counterpoint") and discovers that the music is coming from "a sixteen-inch loudspeaker" (*Conversions*, 67) fixed above the sign.

Entering, he sees "a kind of gallery . . . ten yards wide and forty deep." While waiting for information about the adze, he browses through cases of books until one, a novel by Berthold Auerbach, catches his attention. The reader is then supplied with a translation of "The Otiose Creator," a chapter from this novel, the original German version being given in an appendix. A kind of ironic or paradoxical dream vision of heaven (or hell), the chapter concludes with what seems a non sequitur: "O Maria, hail to the Johnstones! the bloody Johnstones! the fucking Johnstones! the enemies of things as they are! They have come back to their own, they have come back to Alba as kings. May their Gypsy girl have wicked teeth in her cunt!" (*Conversions*, 81).

The narrator is told that he cannot be given information about the adze. He then asks the customs official about the Johnstones mentioned at the end of "The Otiose Creator" and is told that they "are the family of a disowned bastard son of one of the Earls of Mar." This son took the name of Johnstone and pretended "to be not only of noble but of royal blood. . . . He even adopted a coat of arms" (*Conversions*, 83). He then gives the narrator a description of the coat of arms:

Gold a bend silver with halberd gules

and the reason above:

*L'herminette à la taille du roy!* (*Conversions*, 83)

The narrator pursues the topic, and a clerk at the town hall tells him the story of Innocent Johnstone and his discovery of and experiments with fleshmetal, which "destroyed solid materials upon touching them" (*Conversions*, 87). The narrator then finds in the regional archives "a curious document" (*Conversions*, 95), a letter Abendland Johnstone had tried to publish in newspapers around the world from 1745 to 1803, which purports to give a history of the Cult of Sylvius from its beginnings in pagan Italy to its destruction and dispersal in Scotland in 1541. At the end of the letter is a note rejecting Johnstone's account:

Rouen le 10 Brumaire An II

Monsieur,
   Peut-être êtes-vous un bâtard, vous êtes sûrement un imposteur; car
notre dernier roi est mort avant Louis de France. Je veille pour la Reine,
que son règne soit éternel!

LA PLATIÈRE (*Conversions*, 105)

From the letter and the note the narrator concludes that Abe Johnstone
is the stone who was not a king, and so he has answered the first
question.

The narrator decides to go to Rouen and find out who La Platière was
and why he had condemned Johnstone. Before leaving, however, he tries
to visit "Sylvius's Glen," the last home of the Cult, but a "rural policeman" stops him, explaining "that he had orders (he did not say whose) to
keep me out of the glen. Seeing my disappointment . . . he consoled me
with a description of the glen: aside from the waterfall, he said, it was a
plain place, filled with stunted elms and overgrown with unkempt mass-
es of traveller's joy. (I asked what this was; he defined it as a variety of
clematis. I remarked that in my case it was singularly ill-named)"
(*Conversions*, 107).

## The Quest: The Second Question

"What was *La Messe de Sire Fadevant?*"

Before going to Rouen, however, the narrator goes to a library in
Edinburgh to discover what he can about Rolando Lasso, a Renaissance
composer mentioned in the Johnstone letter. He finds no connection
between Lasso and the Sylvian cult or the adze, nor any *La Messe de Sire
Fadevant*. But in the current issue of *Neumata*, a musicological review, he
finds listed for future publication *Una Missa Fa Si Re, Opera Sconosciuta di
Orlando di Lasso*, by Prof. Annibale Bumbè (Siena) and blames himself
"for not recognizing that . . . the mass was one composed on a theme
whose opening notes were *fa*, *si* and *re*, and not one written by or for the
Lord Fadevant" (*Conversions*, 108). The narrator plans to wait for the
published article to appear, but he hears that the Fods are contesting
Wayl's will, and he decides to visit Prof. Bumbè immediately and perhaps gather more evidence for the probate court.

Bumbè tells the narrator that Lasso "let it be known that the three
notes of his motto—*fa*, *si* and *re*—were the abbreviations of secret Latin
words" (*Conversions*, 111). At the time (1571) there was much specula-

tion at court as to what those words might be. Bumbè quotes numerous guesses of the day, three of which Lasso did not reject. Translated from the Latin they are as follows:

> I have made the abbreviation of a king.
> The composer is the prophet of kings.
> Red (if not rouge) marks out the queen. (*Conversions*, 117)

Bumbè's conclusion is that the purpose of the motto was to call attention to a *chanson* by Lasso that contained "a secret message":

> *Fateor Silvium Regem*:
> I acknowledge Silvius as king
>
> *Fata Silvium retexunt*:
> *either* The Fates undo Silvius
> *or* The Fates weave Silvius anew
>
> *Favonius sinistrâ revolvit*:
> The west wind returns on the left (*Conversions*, 116–17)

But Bumbè cannot figure out the reference to a "queen" or who Silvius is or the meaning of the second and third sentences. When the narrator suggests that "*sinistrâ* might indicate bastardy, Dr. Bumbè cut [him] short" (*Conversions*, 118).

## The Quest: The Third Question

"Who shaved the Old Man's Beard?"

The narrator now thinks that he has "a sure answer to the second question of the will, and a probable answer to the first. I had to confirm the latter, and pursue my investigations in the hope that I might come across a clue to the nature of the 'Old Man's Beard'" (*Conversions*, 120). Accordingly, he goes to Rouen, identifies La Platière, and searches the archives of every town in which La Platière lived but comes up with nothing. Finally, he discovers a descendent of La Platière, the painter M. Felix Namque, and visits him in Paris. Felix tells him of a document that might help him that was taken to the United States by Felix's cousin Bunuel Namque-Schlendrian. The narrator has other reasons to return to America: to appear in probate court with his new evidence and

because he "wished to see once more [his] wife, who had recently begun
proceedings against [him] for divorce" (*Conversions*, 128). This is the only
mention of the narrator's wife.

The narrator settles his business with the probate court and his wife
and goes to Hialeah, Florida, where Bunuel Namque-Schlendrian (Bun)
lives. There, after hearing the story of Bun's life (including his early dealings in cowrie shells), he learns that Bun has given the document—a letter from La Platière to a Madame Miot—to a library in Massachusetts.
Before the narrator leaves Hialeah, Bun shows him

> . . . a medieval muleteer's packsaddle that had been given to him by none
> other than Mr. Wayl. I recognized on it a familiar design . . . a naked
> woman stood near the mouth of a stream by a mound of cowrie shells.
> The scene was identical with the one engraved on the point of my adze,
> except that on the saddle the woman was depicted from behind. Mr.
> Wayl had led me to believe that this scene was merely decorative; yet
> here it was underscored with the inscription, *Cypriae Sedes Gloria Regis*,
> while the other side of the saddle bore the arms of the "false Johnstones,"
> with an added mark—a band that crossed the shield from the upper right
> corner to the center and then descended to its point. (*Conversions*, 138)

The narrator journeys to the library. What follows (the next three
chapters) is the narrator's translation of the letter, which purports to give
an account of "a clan of Wallachian Gypsies," the first of whom came to
Scotland in the year 1410: "They had preserved the practice of an old
cult dedicated to Sylvius of Alba Longa, and they worshipped him as a
divine hero, and as their king. In their version of the legend, Sylvius was
no son of Aeneas, but a bastard offspring of Lavinia, fathered by a god
whose name could never be mentioned or written down" (*Conversions*,
141–42). But La Platière knows nothing of the sect before "the establishment of the sect in Scotland, and the first celebrations there of its
mysteries, in a shrine that lay not far from Allova (sic), in the year 1411"
(*Conversions*, 142).

The name Sylvius, the letter goes on to say, not only belonged to the
legendary hero but was also "given as a title to the successive chiefs of
the Gypsies, whom they called kings. They believed that Sylvius was
immortal in the bodies of these kings." In 1411 the Scot Alexander
Stewart, a recent convert, was the king. "Like every king he was born in
bastardy of noble stock; and he had been *chosen*." For Sylvius was not the
supreme ruler; he was the vice-regent of the "'Queen' . . . an obscure
power . . . supposedly a divine being who from time to time, when the

need arose, appeared among her worshippers as a mere woman. . . . Only one of her peculiarities is known: she was nearly always gifted with some Negro blood" (*Conversions*, 142). There follows a description of one of the rites of the sect, the Flaying of the King.

La Platière then tells of the "destruction of Sylvius's shrine. . . . They massacred many of the sect, Gypsy or not. The glen was ravaged, its spring polluted, its sacred tree cut to bits, its royal stone smashed, even its thriving vines uprooted" (*Conversions*, 148). The Queen, who led the glen's defense, was taken prisoner and sent to Rome for trial. She was condemned as a witch but was allowed to present her case to Pope Pius II. A transcription of the confrontation between Queen and Pope is then given, followed by a description of her torture and execution. Though the Pope tells her, "You will hang and not burn; yours is a common offense," he relents and "at the end of the trial minutes the verdict reads (although the Queen was already dead): *Convicta et combusta*" (*Conversions*, 151, 153). Since the massacre the history of the sect "has been a sad one: fits of enthusiasm fading into long wastes of abandonment. In our century the apathy of the believers has been such that the Barilone of Massa may fall into ruin" (*Conversions*, 155).

Finally, he describes his "ensuring the perpetuation of the Queen's monument. Last week I traveled with it by land as far as Houlgate, there hiring a small fishingboat, which I took out myself, desiring to conceal the nature and destination of my cargo. After rowing for several hours . . . I spied a small island. . . . Several hundred yards from the center of its southern shore I sank the memorial of the Queen in the sea" (*Conversions*, 156).

Following the letter, its author unidentified, is a parenthetical note: "(Ten days later Roland [i.e., La Platière], learning of his wife's execution, wandered from Rouen several miles into the countryside, and after pinning to his breast a scrawled explanation of his act, killed himself near Bourg-Beaudoin. He is buried on the spot. Aside from the information it contains, his letter is curious for being addressed to Madame Miot; he had attended the burial of her ashes three years before)" (*Conversions*, 157).

The narrator thinks that La Platière's letter has given him the answer to the will's third question, which he relates to Miss Dryrein, the executrix of Wayl's will, but she dismisses his answer "with a simple No." She shows the narrator a movie, taken by Mr. Wayl and narrated by Isidore Fod, of the "Barilone, that strange underground palace unearthed this summer near Massa Marittima, west of Siena": "Its walls are covered with interesting frescoes. Here is a sample of them. In the leftmost of these three paintings we see a clearing ringed with vine-covered trees. A group of vagabonds attacks a gathering of gentlefolk at a sumptuous outdoor banquet. In the right-hand painting we have the same scene after the attackers have left—the ground covered with the bodies of the slain, the trees cut down or burned: no living thing, animal or plant, remains. Unfortunately the middle space has been badly damaged, and one cannot see what happens there" (*Conversions*, 160).

After the movie ends and Miss Dryrein turns on the lights, she "looked at me questioningly; but I did not understand. She shook her head resignedly, and her attention to my predicament ebbed augustly" (*Conversions*, 160).

The narrator visits the Massa "a few months later." He examines the "middle" fresco of Mr. Wayl's movie with a flashlight: "All I found was the outline of certain tendrils near the bottom of the picture, one of which bore the remains of greenish-white coloring; reaching down from above, a hand clutched the tendrils."

The narrator asks his guide "to identify the subjects of the 'middle' fresco and the one over it. Asked who the sanctimonious bishop was, he said:

> *Che grillo*! Amen.
> Of the stoned woman: *Che pazzia*! Amen.
> Of the plants in the 'middle' fresco: *Alba*! Amen." (*Conversions*, 162–63)

In a rage of anger and frustration the narrator grabs the man by the throat, knocks him on the head with his flashlight, and flees, "weeping with shame and disappointment." The next day the narrator realizes that the man's "answers were not the impertinences I had taken them to be. What I had heard as *Che grillo*! and (forgetting the position of the tonic accent) *Che pazzia*! had surely been *Cirillo* and *Ipazia*, protagonists in just such a scene as that fresco portrayed. Had he perhaps meant something else too by *Alba*?" (*Conversions*, 163).

In the final chapter the narrator, with the help of a group of amateur skindivers, finds the monument that La Platière sank in the sea. On the morning of that day he learns that La Platière's letter has been declared a forgery and that as a result "Mr. Wayl's will had been thrown out as a complete hoax; and that Beatrice and Isidore Fod were to inherit the fortune. I had promptly decided to fight these decisions. Now . . . I found my confidence waning" (*Conversions*, 165). On the boat he goes over in his mind all that he has discovered and sees that it could all have been an elaborate hoax. "As to why [Wayl] should play such an elaborate trick on me, I was at a loss—a modest if dilettantish mulatto hardly seemed prey worthy of such trouble. Yet I felt that I had, at the end of long folly, reached the sad truth, the truth of my delusion. As we hunted the rough Atlantic floor, I was sure we should find nothing" (*Conversions*, 166).

But he does find something: "A thumb-shaped structure, six feet high and four feet thick, rested on the seafloor, a clocklike mechanism forming the greater part of its mass" (*Conversions*, 167). There follows a description of what might be called a perpetual motion machine—an astounding lunar clock driven by the backward and forward motion of generations of herring, the description of which is too long to quote (six pages) and impossible to paraphrase or condense. And on a flat surface at the top of the clock he saw the following:

> [T]wo figures, perhaps six inches high. One was a man, white, naked except for a crown of little faded leaves. The other was a black woman, also naked. The man was caught in a net of tangled white wire. Their features and limbs were carved crudely, except for the woman's vulva, which had been carefully represented as a mouth, with red tonguetip protruding between tiny sharp teeth. With one hand she lifted one of her breasts; with the other she held out a minute golden adze to the trapped king, who stretched his hands toward her.
>
> On an exterior metal band that separated this scene from the panel of moons, two words had been roughly scratched: *Mundorys Lorsea*. (*Conversions*, 171)

The narrator believes that the moon clock had "failed to yield the third answer" and decides to end his quest. "My long search had consumed more than the little money I had once possessed—I had even had to pawn the adze. There was nothing for me to do but return home and begin paying my debts" (*Conversions*, 171).

## Stories, Digressions, and Style

What I have given, a bare bones account of the narrator's search, is, even more than most paraphrases, misleading. That search, leading as it does to the partial unraveling of the mystery of the Cult of Sylvius, makes up the main plot of the novel. But much of the novel is taken up with other matters, for out of the narrator's travels evolve a number of "stories," fascinating in their own right, maybe digressions, maybe not.

The "minor novelist," for example, before he tells the narrator how he won the adze, gives a paraphrase of his latest novel: three strangers, brought together through their love of music, are involved in an airplane crash in Greenland. In their struggle to survive, two are killed, and the third wanders over the ice until he dies as well. This story takes up 12 pages, its only seeming connection with the main plot being the song the final survivor sings just before he dies.

When early in his quest the narrator visits Beatrice Fod, we are told of her discovery of a sexual position that maximizes pleasure while absolutely preventing conception. This discovery one would think a boon to mankind but in fact the authorities, religious and secular, join forces to prevent the discovery from being revealed. Her brother Isidore Fod also seems to bring a great gift to mankind when he discovers an ingenious method for combating a plague, but it turns out that his "cure" ultimately makes the plague much worse. It's difficult to see what these stories have to do with the main plot.

Likewise, it is not easy to see what the stories of the "notorious gang boss" Allen Cavallo, who tries to market drug-infused cactus spines only to fall on them and into pitiful suffering before he dies, the account of the Panarchist Uprising of 1911, and the recording of the languages of the Voe-Doge brothers have to do with the main plot. A sample of the language follows:

> Lop oh oh kop, Eftas was saying, yoppo you boploppo oh dopyop foppo ohlop, ee voppeenop top hoppo you gop hop mopyop boppeye roptop hop moppay. . . .
>
> Naraguts tarago yaragou, baragag-haraguead, answered Gore: twaraguins aragare twaraguins aragand naragueitharaguer haragas praraguiaragoraraguitaraguy. (*Conversions*, 64)

Much of the important Scotland chapters is taken up with the inverted paradise of "The Otiose Creator" and with an account of Innocent Johnstone's disastrous obsession with fleshmetal, involving the accidental discovery of the significance of farts produced in a maid by mumbleberries.

In fact, all Felix Namque tells the narrator is that he should go to Florida to see Felix's cousin. The rest of his chapter is taken up with an explanation of the working of the "machine" he uses to produce his paintings. His cousin Bun shows the narrator the curious packsaddle and sends him to a library in Massachusetts. The rest of this rather long chapter recounts his life story, nothing of which, except for the cowries and the names of a few of the horses, would seem to have much to do with the cult of Sylvius or the queen or the three questions.

What partially binds all these "stories" together is, of course, the narrator's quest, but even here there is a subtle twist, for the quest in *The Conversions* operates on at least two levels: the narrator's attempt to solve three riddles, the answers to which will earn him a fortune; and the reader's search to discover the truth about the narrator. The reader is engaged on both levels, the narrator, seemingly, on only one. The novel, then, employs a dramatic irony common to much modernist fiction, that of the "unreliable narrator."

And perhaps just as important as the narrator's quest is Mathews's dislocating of perspective, a frustration of conventional expectations that begins subtly in the first chapter. *The Conversions* opens with the following short paragraphs:

> The wealthy amateur Grent Wayl invited me to his New York house for an evening's diversion. Welcoming me, he said: The cheek of our Bea! pointing to his niece, Miss Beatrice Fod, who, accompanied on the harmonium by her brother Isidore, sang to the assembled guests.
>
> > At night when you're asleep
> > > Without no pants on
> > Into your tent I'll creep
> > > Without no pants on
>
> Such nervous speech! Why should he mind, since the song delighted the company? Mr. Wayl was aging, aging; but no one would take his words lightly. (*Conversions*, 3–4)

Why did Wayl invite the narrator? What is the nature of the relationship between them? How long have they known each other? "Wealthy amateur" hints at Wayl's social and economic position and prepares us for his erudition and eccentricities. Beyond that, we learn that he is "aging, aging," that he has a niece and nephew and a harmonium. Since the word "diversion" is not placed within quotation marks, we must assume that it is the narrator's characteristic way of speaking, which indicates that he is a part of the world of wealthy amateurs in New York City, whatever his relationship to Wayl might be. The exclamation marks are ambiguous. Either Mr. Wayl and the narrator are playing a game, playing parts in a little drama, or they are very easily excited. If the exclamation marks are placed against the word "cheek," one might think the former, but when the narrator remarks that "no one would take his words lightly," we begin to think that Wayl may be having some fun at the expense of a somewhat uncomfortable visitor.

Mr. Wayl then takes the narrator "upstairs" and shows him a "ritual adze," one side of which is "chased with wiry engravings," seven in all, six depicting a woman whose face is "crosshatched for swarthiness." That Wayl should reveal the adze in secret and that the narrator would use such a word as "chased" support what follows, the suggestion that the narrator is learned in such matters: speculating that the woman was a "heroine or saint . . . Mr. Wayl asked me to interpret the series of engravings" (*Conversions*, 4).

The narrator's response mixes precise description of the engravings with a Christian interpretation that obviously doesn't please Wayl, who "exclaimed: You're as dumb as is!" (*Conversions*, 5). For the narrator, people "exclaim" things, a word which confirms our previous impression of him, and Wayl's "You're as dumb as is!" makes us take his "The cheek of our Bea!" more seriously. And the narrator seems to take Wayl's choice, "heroine or saint," as a command and chooses the latter, though even at the time he realizes that the first and last scenes don't fit or have to be forced into a Christian interpretation. Obviously, Wayl knows the proper interpretation.

This short opening chapter closes as follows:

> Excuse me, sir, I said, if your pleasure was marred.
> He was suddenly friendly: No one with purple eyes is stupid. But do you have perfect pitch?
> I answered that I had. Leaving the library, he took the adze with him.
> (*Conversions*, 5)

The phrase "your pleasure was marred" completes the reader's impression of the narrator, and Wayl's alternation between impatience and friendliness confirms one's sense that he expects something of the narrator, a belief further enforced by the mysterious non sequitur "do you have perfect pitch?" which leads back to the song at the beginning and the harmonium. The last sentence's abruptness echoes the opening sentence.

As is generally true of good writing, one hardly notices the cleverness of the style of this opening chapter of Mathews's first novel, a style that combines a concern for the reader with a refusal to condescend. The situation described—a man invites another to a drawing room party—is realistic, but the language throws the realism slightly askew. The opening here would seem to be a better example of what John Ash says about the opening of *Tlooth*, that it shows an "affinity" with the opening of a novel by Ronald Firbank (Ash, 21). Like Firbank, Mathews creates a world in which all the parts are "representational," but when put together they come to "represent" something other than what the reader expects. Such a style causes the frustrated reader either to give up or to pay closer attention, not to what is signified but to what is actually being described, what is actually happening. Mathews's style is both limpid and opaque in that there is nothing difficult about the "stories" that make up the novel but how (or if) those stories go together presents great difficulty.

## Panaceas and Reversals

A reader steeped in modernist literature is quite likely to seize upon the significance of the seven scenes on the adze, believing that the interpretation of those scenes will be important. And indeed it is. Mathews says that "the substratum of those first three novels is religious," and the scenes on the adze begin the "sort of white goddess legend" (Tillman, 35; *Way Home*, 156) that lies at the heart of the quest. But more subtle, and in the long run perhaps more important, is the introduction of the other main themes or motifs of the novel—music, games, pain and sex, reversal, family (blood). As is characteristic of the style, Mathews sets them up in an oblique, glancing way. The narrator and Wayl begin a "game" involving mythological interpretation, the woman on the adze (a cutting tool) appears "outside a burning grove" within which are "many tormented figures," Bea sings a bawdy song accompanied by her brother Isidore on a drawing room instrument.

Take, for example, the way Wayl's dismissal of the narrator's seemingly learned interpretation of the scenes on the adze begins a pattern of what might be called reversal, a pattern continued in Scotland when beautiful music is heard in "indirect proportion to the fineness of the weather: it needs a truly foul day to hear the music fair." And in Barilone there is the grasshopper doorbell: when the grasshoppers fall silent Sig. Fesso knows that someone is at the door. It seems that Bea's "position" can end the population problem, that Is's technique would be the way to stop an epidemic, that "fleshmetal" will solve the thorniest problems concerned with composition of matter, that Felix has discovered a foolproof way for the artist to create without the aid of inspiration or luck. But the Fods' solutions turn out to be disasters, fleshmetal is uncontrollable, and the intricate system and machine used by Felix don't determine the work of art. This pattern of reversal culminates in the apparently useless perpetual motion machine at the end of the novel.

The reversals in turn sometimes deal with pain and suffering, thus introducing the medical and disease motif that Mathews makes even more use of in *Tlooth*. Here we have the epidemic and the grotesquely drugged Cavallo and, again anticipating *Tlooth* in a humorous way, "truth dentists." The fifth chapter, "The Sores," is a tale of the suffering of three men, the only survivors of an airplane crash in Greenland. The men are first brought together by their love of old German music, and the last of the men dies singing about a "farmer's girl" who was a "queen" who slept with an "emperor" who "died the next day," which takes us back to Bea and the harmonium and the scenes on the adze. This suffering motif ties in not only with the "religious substructure" but also with the intricate use of music that pervades the novel.

## The Narrator and the Reader

Taken together, these and numerous other patterns[2] seem to intertwine around a central character to produce a picaresque novel about a man who wanders about the United States and Europe in search of information that will win him a fortune. But as we come to realize that the narrator is involved in something more than this search, he becomes something more than merely a unifying device. By the end of the novel we congratulate ourselves on having figured out who he is and that his real failure lies not in his losing the fortune but in his not realizing, as we do, his true identity. Thus the reader is somewhat compensated for the disappointment of not having the last riddle solved for him: in the best tradition of modernism the failure to solve the riddle emphasizes the more important failure of the narrator to discover who he is, a failure that returns him to a mundane life of paying debts.

Our "interpretation" is supported by the little we know about the narrator. He seems to be desperate, not simply for money but for fabulous sums of money (a point I explain below), his wife is divorcing him, and he is a mulatto. He is somewhat learned, knowledgeable in music, and obviously used to libraries and research and scholarly investigation. Putting all this together we can invent a number of scenarios. For example: the narrator is what he calls himself, a "modest if dilettantish mulatto," a fearful hanger-on in the society of wealthy amateurs who wrecks his life (goes into debt, loses his wife) trying to win a fortune he never could have won in the first place. Or since, as he himself says, he "hardly seemed prey worthy of such trouble," the narrator is a petty con man in fashionable society who winds up getting what he deserves without ever realizing, so blinded is he by his greed, who he really is. Or the fact that he is a mulatto not only is relevant to the Cult of Sylvius but also introduces an alienation at the end somewhat in the way that at the end of *Tlooth* we learn . . .

Or so it seems. Carried away as we are by our cleverness, we are likely not to notice, much less find significance in, the fact that the first word in *The Conversions*, excluding the article, is "wealthy" until in contemplating the novel we remember that its last word (excluding the appendices) is "debts." Then we might begin to consider more carefully the narrator, a man who actually seems to have plenty of money (he attends Wayl's party, he travels continually around Europe and back and forth between the United States and Europe, he pays historians to do research for him). Though according to Mathews, the narrator is "reduced to a point of total fearfulness" (Tillman, 34), his quest for the answer to the riddles seems more the result of his love of the challenge than his desire for the inheritance. He pursues the mystery of the adze before he knows about the will, and he turns down huge sums of money offered for it by Bea and Is. At the very most he seems to want *more* money, it being very unlikely that a fearful man of modest means would turn down a million dollars before he learns that the adze might be worth much more. Yet at the end we discover that he has "even had to pawn the adze" in an attempt to pay his debts, debts resulting from the travel expenses of a man who a few months earlier turned down a million dollars.

Mathews says, "The first two novels [*The Conversions* and *Tlooth*] have only one character, the narrators, both of them distraught with their obsessions" (Interview). I assume that on one level at least the narrator of *The Conversions* is distraught because of a material obsession, the desire for the fortune. Yet as we have seen, he doesn't seem to be much interested in wealth at the beginning, and he continues his quest even after he knows that solving the last riddle probably won't win him the prize.

At this point we might want to ask ourselves two questions: Why has the narrator written his story and for whom has he written it? The second question is the key to the first. Who has added the appendices? Where are the footnotes signaled on pages 146, 149, 151, 167 (and possibly 145)? Now there is a reason for the abrupt opening and closing: perhaps we have only a part of a longer work, a fragment (the footnotes begin at number 4). Perhaps we, the readers, find that, like the narrator, we have been laboring under an illusion, have taken the part for the whole. Then, when we remember that the narrator must have written his book after he started "paying his debts," we realize that the fragment we are reading must be part of a whole from which the narrator we once felt so superior to (or someone else, the effect is the same) has removed . . . what?

Of course, we can never know for sure. And this is the more important unsolved riddle, of which the other riddles were only a part. When Mathews asserts, as he has on several occasions, that figuring out the answer to the last riddle, "Who shaved the Old Man's Beard?" doesn't "solve" everything, either for the narrator or the reader, he is not merely defending himself against the charge of "cheating" the reader; he is hinting, I think, at another "story," one to which all these other stories run. But since Mathews doesn't tell us that story,[3] it would seem that the charge of cheating has simply been moved to another level.

Or has it? Finally, Mathews may be inventing enough to make possible an act of creation on the part of the reader. The two "facts" that constitute the "keys" to the two levels of the novel—the solving of the third riddle and the revelation that the narrator is a mulatto—actually complete the establishment of a framework that the reader must fill in (or complete), a framework that may include the reader not only as creator but also as character. Thus Mathews is justifiably annoyed (Ash, 27) when a translator cannot see, first, the ambiguity of the arbitrariness of the narrator being a mulatto and, second, the fact that this revelation should come at the end, not for its "shock" value but because it turns the reader back into the text and makes him begin his act of creation. For up to this point the reader has been "interpreting."

From our critical perspective we can see why, though well enough received, *The Conversions* didn't make much of an impact in the literary climate of the early 1960s: not only did it seem to lack the "commitment" and "compassion" reviewer and critics expected but it also was genuinely original in its shifting of the problem of closure from the writer to the reader. For those readers who prefer it, there *is* an ending in the modernist tradition of the unreliable narrator, an ending grounded in irony. But the novel subtly transcends this level and opens into another narrative, one that depends upon the reader for its completion. The final "conversion" is that of the reader, which causes him to go back and reconsider (and reread) the book he thought he had finished. This is a technique that Mathews develops even further in his next novel, *Tlooth*.

## Chapter Four

# More Conversions: *Tlooth*

### The Pursuit of Revenge

In the previous chapter we saw how Mathews uses the plot as a frame for other stories and games. If anything Mathews intensifies this technique in *Tlooth*. In *The Conversions*, from the time of the reading of the will, at least, the reader, in spite of what seems to be a number of digressions, some of them long, never loses sight of the narrator's quest for the answers to the three questions and the unfolding of the Cult of Sylvius that grows from it. In *Tlooth*, however, we hardly grasp, at first, what the nature of the quest is, and for long periods it seems to drop out of the novel altogether.

As is typical with Mathews, the action begins abruptly, in this instance during a baseball game being played in a Russian prison camp between the Fideists and the Defective Baptists. The narrator (whose full name we don't discover until almost the end of the novel), the catcher for the Defective Baptists, substitutes a ball rigged with a small explosive device while Evelyn Roak is at bat: "I expected the explosion to create general confusion, stun and knock down the batter, and explain the batter's death. The bomb itself would kill no one, but I had concealed in my right shin guard, ready to use as soon as the ball had been detonated, a hypodermic of botulin."[1]

Roak is a surgeon, and, apparently, the narrator seeks revenge because in removing a "troublesome spur of bone" Roak also removed "the index and ring fingers of my left hand. I was then a violinist" (*Tlooth*, 187). But the plot fails because of a wild pitch.

The narrator, who has been in the camp for two years and has tried previously to kill Roak, explains: "The organization of the camp was sectarian. On arrival, prisoners were arbitrarily and finally committed to the Americanist, Darbyist, Defective Baptist, Fideist or Resurrectionist division" (*Tlooth*, 191). The narrator, refusing to join the camp orchestra, band, or choir, is assigned to the dental infirmary and works for a woman dentist, Dr. Zarater. They both have an interest in the work of

King Dri, "the 'Philosopher-Dentist'." After an account of how Dr. Dri made his great discovery, the narrator summarizes it:

> The human body . . . is not a single organism made of constituent parts, but an assemblage of entities on whose voluntary collaboration the func- tioning of the whole depends. . . . Every entity within the body is endowed with its own psyche, more or less developed in awareness and self-consciousness. . . . Health exists when the various entities are happy, for they then perform their roles properly and co-operate with one anoth- er. Disease appears when some member of the organism rejects its voca- tion. Medicine intervenes to bring the wayward member back to its place in the body's society. At best the heart makes its own medicine, convinc- ing the rebel of its love by addressing it sympathetically; but a doctor is often needed to abet the communion of heart and member, and some- times, when the patient has surrendered to unconsciousness or despair, to speak for the heart itself. (*Tlooth*, 194)

Thus, as a dentist Dr. Dri tries to persuade an infected tooth to accept its vocation and come back into happy harmony with the whole. If this cannot be done, he convinces the tooth to come out and leave the organ- ism of its own accord.

While a dental assistant the narrator meets the beautiful Yana, with whom Roak is in love, and begins to work through her to achieve revenge, first sending presents of candy to Roak through Yana. Six are harmless, but the seventh is filled with a highly corrosive substance. When Roak comes to the dental clinic, however, it is Dr. Zarater who examines her and handles the case. So the narrator loses another chance for revenge.

The narrator's severed fingers have not healed properly. They are sore, and when pimples begin to appear, the camp doctor, Dr. Amset, diag- noses syphilis, but his cure is ineffective.

Roak is released from prison, and the narrator, in order to pursue her, joins three other inmates in an escape plan. The quartet enters a vehicle in the "'home-made animal' race," so called because the vehicles entered must have the shape of an animal. During the race they break away, out- run their pursuers to a nearby mountain range, abandon their vehicle (useless in the mountains), and begin a long trek to Afghanistan.

Part 2 of the novel (42 pages) is taken up with the story of that trek. Alternating between notebook accounts of the journey and autobio- graphical tales of the escapees, this section seems to have very little to do with the revenge plot. So little, in fact, that one tends to forget about

Roak. They hike over mountains and through passes, forage for food, endure miserable weather. There are accounts of encounters with tribes. During the journey one person, Hapi, dies. The other three make it ultimately to Kabul where, ill and exhausted, they recuperate in a hospital.

Part 3 begins with the narrator, still in Kabul, discovering that Roak is in Venice. Health "shattered" by "exhaustion and disease," the narrator nonetheless goes to Venice. "Before leaving Afghanistan, I suffered the first of many spells of dizziness and hallucination. Our doctors, attributing it to fatigue, found no remedy. They were as unsuccessful in treating my hand. A Wassermann test confirmed Dr. Amset's diagnosis" (*Tlooth*, 288).

Not surprisingly, then, the narrator, upon arriving in Venice, collapses. Eyes throbbing, stumps of fingers itching, unable to sleep, the narrator spends a week in the hospital, behind shutters to keep out the light. While there she meets Vetullio Smautf, "the half-brother of the present Countess Mur della Marsa" (*Tlooth*, 290). I say "she," for it is in this section that one begins to wonder about the sex of the narrator (the assumption of most readers to this point would be that the narrator is a man), but it is only late in the novel, if then, that the reader becomes certain. We also learn at this point that the narrator's last name is Allant. Through Smautf she meets the Count Mur della Marsa. Finding that she is out of work, he asks her to write a scenario for a blue film he is going to produce for which, if he accepts it, he will pay $9000. While she considers the offer, a messenger named Joan brings the Count a package. The Count invites the narrator to his palace (Palazzo Zen), and after he has gone, Joan tells her the story of the Count: "The Count was a plebian Frenchman called René Washux, a dancer, some say a female impersonator, in the 'Mirror Fantasy' troupe of the Casino de Paris. . . . [The Countess] fell in love with Washux on sight. . . . Washux accepted her in exchange for her title and half her fortune. . . . [H]e has never once made love to the Countess. No one knows why. Is he impotent? His sexual escapades are notorious, even if their exact nature is unclear. Has he other physical defects? . . . Is he homosexual?" (*Tlooth*, 292).

One of the family properties is a stretch of bogland said to conceal an oracle, and nearby stands "a Fideist chapel. Attendance at it is a rare distinction. The Count has the hereditary right to keep out whomever he wishes. . . . I believe your cousin [Roak] was given the privilege, surprising for a newcomer" (*Tlooth*, 293).

The narrator begins "the scenario of the Count's film, working with an energy that only my intermittent hallucinations could stifle" (*Tlooth*, 293).

Over the course of the next three chapters the narrator attends a party at the Palazzo Zen, has dinner with Smautf, and witnesses his funeral. These actual events are interwoven with scenes from the scenario for the blue film, and reality and fantasy shade into and out of each other in a more or less surreal way. Such confusion is most likely the result of the narrator's physical condition, her hallucinations.

The Count turns down the narrator's scenario, and the narrator almost despairs because she believes she may have lost access to the chapel and her chance to catch up with Roak. But "certain smiles of the Count had suggested another means of winning him, simpler, more promising, more hazardous. . . . I . . . knelt down by him. His hands touched my bent neck ; and a few minutes afterward . . . I knew that my instinct had been true. . . . The 'Count' lay inert by my side. I tried to shake 'him' into wakefulness. I had solved the riddle of his marital chastity" (*Tlooth*, 320–21). And she now calls him *Renée* rather than *René*. As a result of the affair he has promised to take her to his Mestre estate where the chapel and also an oracle are located, but at this point the narrator discovers that Roak has left Italy and gone to India.

They make the trip to the Mestre estate and the oracle anyway. The Count tells her: "'Here's what you do: take the boot off your right foot, and your sock if you're wearing one, and stick your leg in up to the knee. Keep it there for a minute plus eight seconds . . . then remove it quickly. The prophecy will follow.'" Her foot sinks in the mud, and after she pulls it out, she kneels. "In a moment there was perhaps a liquid murmur or rumble and out of the ooze, as if a capacious ball of sound had forced its passage to the air, a voice distinctly gasped, 'Tlooth'" (*Tlooth*, 323).

Six weeks later the narrator secures a position as a nurse's aide on a WHO medical team and, continuing her pursuit of Roak, leaves for India.

In part 4 the narrator moves from India to Morocco, back to Italy, then to France. As in part 2, it's difficult to see what much of the action has to do with the main plot. In India, for example, the narrator discovers that she cannot get to Bombay, where Roak is. Most of the chapter is taken up with a bizarre tale and an account of a flood, and at the end of the adventure the narrator discovers that Roak has left India for North Africa. In Morocco she discovers that after leaving the cryptic note, "*traîne, pleure, aigus*" (*Tlooth*, 337), Roak has returned to Italy, and most of this chapter is taken up with the fantastic tale of a dancer who dances herself to death.

Back in Italy (Atri) the narrator encounters an American doctor (Nathaniel Cavesenough), who accidentally (?) snags her with a fish hook, examines her hand, and declares that she has yaws, not syphilis. He then tells her that Roak is in an Atri museum to "see the coins before they're removed. 'Hadrian's Angels'—it turns out they're fakes" (*Tlooth*, 341). She goes through the museum (there is a significant description of it) looking for Roak and winds up beneath it in a cheese cellar. "Evelyn Roak appeared at the far end of a row of cheeses, walking toward me. The afternoon had been too much for my empty stomach and harassed mind. Bitter fumes swirled into me, I fell senselessly toward the blue flags of the cellar floor" (*Tlooth*, 344).

The narrator awakes in a hotel in the Alps in Savoy where she learns that through the cooperation of Cavesenough and Roak she has been sent to Dr. D—— to be cured of the yaws. While resting for a week at the hotel, she once again meets the Count's messenger in Venice, Joan, who agrees to stay with her for a while. Dr. D—— takes her to an old *rhabilleuse*, who applies a rough treatment of folk medicine, which cures her of her disease.

In part 5 the narrator (now identified as Nephthys Mary Allant) marries Joan. She learns that Roak was in Atri because she is involved in the business of selling pet nightingales, which are caught in traps baited with cattails. "But not ordinary cattails: only those half-rotted by the tiny worms that are found in Atrian cheese" (*Tlooth*, 353). Dr. D—— then tells her that Roak suffers from "a perilous condition, brought on by bad teeth. The body's normal production of antibodies has been permanently upset. . . . For Dr. Roak the risk is exposure to a serious disease when already subject to infection. . . . [T]he infection would exhaust the antibody reaction, leaving nothing for the disease, and the rest would be up to the undertaker" (*Tlooth*, 353–54).

The narrator resumes her dental instruction in a town not far from Lyon. "The marshes surrounding the town hold the richest growth of cattails in Europe or Africa" (*Tlooth*, 355). Roak visits her there, saying that she has come to make up. The narrator examines Roak's teeth. "Please to notice my lower left molars and the small canyon made by your candy-bomb—idiot!" The narrator is "ready to satisfy [her] patience—gas, straps, and drills were at hand." But she notices a "slight swelling" and is "sure that an abscess had formed under the gold of Evelyn's damaged teeth" (*Tlooth*, 358). Roak's forehead is "hot and dry," and she has just returned from Sfax, where there is a small-pox epidemic. The narrator realizes that Roak has contracted the disease. She tells her only that her gum is irritated and gives her an inadequate dose of antibiotic. "Then I relinquished my opponent to her stars" (*Tlooth*, 359).

The novel ends with a very detailed description of "a print of Sfax, a belated *image d'Epinal*" (*Tlooth*, 359) that hangs over the narrator's office door.

*Tlooth*, then, traces the narrator's pursuit of Evelyn Roak from a Russian prison camp (possibly in Georgia[2]) to Kabul, then from Kabul to Venice to Milan to India to Morocco to Rome to France, where revenge, such as it is, is finally accomplished. Thus the work is, on one level, a traditional action/suspense novel employing the primitive unifying device of the road story. But anyone who has read the novel knows that this description is not only inadequate but misleading as well.

## Best-Laid Plans

The novel opens with a failed attempt at revenge and closes with a refusal to take revenge. It opens as what seems to be a science fiction novel or a political satire and closes in a realistic framework. Its principle throughout, frantic movement, is frozen at the end in a detailed description of a painting. The novel is similar to *The Conversions* and not only in form and technique. Dentistry is introduced almost at once, the "Old Man's Beard" is alluded to in an early chapter (by a doctor who likes "to give at least two names to things" [*Tlooth*, 100]), the escapees rest in a glen of "silver firs," someone is reading a back issue of *The Worm Runners Digest*. And at the end Bea Fod turns up. The first chapter of *Tlooth*, like that of *The Conversions*, "sets up" the novel (one suspects a game that takes us from "the sense behind the sound" of "Fur bowls!" to the painting at the end). But as in *The Conversions* the style, the rhythm of the prose, seems a little off, not something the ear is used to,[3] and the reader is likely not to pick up at once on the fact that disease, religion, and mystery are important, let alone the significance of the sex of the umpire (or of the abbreviation "Ump") and why it is significant that the novel opens with a game. The reader will be trying to figure out why there is a Soviet prison camp called "Jacksongrad" and what Darbyists and Americanists are (even if he doesn't have to look up Fideist and Resurrectionist). The opening, then, in disorienting readers, not only mystifies them but shakes them out of reading (responding to the text) "realistically."

Thus the novel at first seems a repetition of *The Conversions*, the quest here being for revenge rather than riches. Mathews introduces the revenge motif in the opening chapter when the narrator tells us of Evelyn Roak's having ruined the narrator's career as a violinist through a botched operation. Significantly, however, this motive is given in a footnote as a kind of digression from the ingenious description of a booby-trapped baseball, and the reader is much more interested in the method of revenge than in either the revenge itself or the reason for it. The opening chapter sets the pattern of the novel: again and again design dissolves in detail until finally the novel itself moves (metaphorically) out of the temporal sphere and into a "print of Sfax, a belated *image d'Epinal.*"

We should bear in mind that the narrator is a musician turned dental assistant and Mathews appears to work in the modernist tradition of relative point of view; but the narrator possesses so much information on so many diverse subjects that she becomes almost an omniscient voice. Not entirely, however. The effect is that by the end of the second section of the novel the reader senses that the narrator is not limited by participation in the action yet still accepts the ignorance of the narrator as regards the movements of Roak. This modulation of narrative voice is central in that it denies the possibility of "interpreting" the action from even one perspective, no matter how "relative" that perspective might be. Such an ambiguous combination of authority and play is a major characteristic of Mathews's fiction. His narrators display what probably would be implausible erudition if we knew more about them (as it is, we tend to think that there is no reason why they *shouldn't* know what they know); but the erudition often collapses in futility. The point seems to be not that this or that scheme or word game is pointless, but pointlessness itself (see Interview), a pointlessness that, in *Tlooth*, operates on two levels, echoing the tiered structure of *The Conversions*.

To begin, we have the going awry of one best-laid plan after another (similar to the motif of reversal in *The Conversions*). The bomb plot fails when the ball-bomb rolls harmlessly away into a drain. The caramel candy plot, while it does some damage to Roak's teeth, does not deliver her into the hands of the narrator (at least not immediately). Another familiar device is the elaborate digression: an "explanation" of why Roak's group is called "the sugars" that involves an ingenious smuggling plot; the story of a census of a nearby region that results in wholesale death and destruction, causing one of the census takers to observe, "A census that alters the size of the population it studies is a deadly absurdity" (*Tlooth*, 222). The reader assumes that these digressions will somehow or other be "thematic," or at least tangentially connected to the main plot. But so entertaining are the digressions that the reader doesn't mind, even when such connections are not made.

## Physical and Spiritual: Medicine and Sects

The novel, then, though it deals with revenge, has no "message," no "moral" in any conventional sense. What it seems to insist upon from the very beginning is that the parts of a novel are to the novel what the novel is to life—inessential. That is, art is not life, is not "necessary" to life. But art is necessary to a certain kind of living, to an existence beyond that of the purely animal, and just as we are "entertained" by a novel, so we are "entertained" by all the novels within the novel *Tlooth*. Setting up the revenge motif only to deemphasize it is but a major example of the effect throughout: a forcing of the reader out of his preconceived ideas about fiction. The reader thinks he should find the "theme" of the novel at the beginning, and he thinks he has been clever when he locates it in the footnote. Likewise, the reader thinks that motivation must be connected with the groups that inhabit the camp: Fideists and Defective Baptists and Darbyists and Americanists. And how, one wonders, does the medical motif that is established in the dental episode early on relate to the religious/revenge theme that seems so appropriate to a Russian concentration camp?

So when Evelyn Roak (after surviving another attempt on her life) leaves the camp and the narrator decides to escape in order to pursue her, the novel seems to be coming together in the way it should, and soon the various "themes" that have been introduced will begin to cohere. What follows, however, is an elaborate description of an elaborate method of escape involving clever mechanical animal-shaped vehicles and a word puzzle. The puzzle, the kind of word game that Mathews is fond of and that occurs in the novel in less obvious ways, is, I think, the key to the opening of the novel. It exists for its own sake, and trying to figure it out is fascinating but illuminates nothing. Similarly, the first chapters of the novel, while supposedly concerned with the conflict between the narrator and Roak, have actually been taken up with self-contained schemes—the bomb attempt, the candy plot, the escape plan. Moreover, Dr. Dri's philosophical dentistry, which mixes tooth pulling with metaphysics, suggests the fruitlessness of trying to find meaning in what has been developed purely for pleasure. (Of course, the concern with dentistry reaches a humorous culmination in the word that provides the title of the novel.)

But, characteristically, the various stories and digressions do cohere. The novel actually begins with a quotation from Hippocrates: "It is a mistake to regard one disease as more divine than another, since all is human and all divine" (*Tlooth*, 186). Now clearly the quotation is related to the novel's disease motif. But just as relevant is the second part of the quotation, "all is human and all divine." Mathews says, "The substratum of those first three novels is a religious one" (Tillman, 35), and his use of various sects (Fideist, Resurrectionists, Darbyists, etc.) emphasizes somewhat subtly the crucial relationship between the physical and the spiritual as well as the relationship between reason and faith. Mathews points to the "Nestorian heresy," which is developed in the "Spires and Squares" chapter (Tillman, 35). Nestorius was, as regards orthodox Christianity, a heretic in his assertion that the divine and human remained separate in Christ. Fideists believe that faith is necessary to the discovery of truth (though they divide in their attitudes toward reason). By Resurrectionists Mathews may mean a sect centered in some way on the resurrection of the flesh, but he probably knows that the term was applied to grave robbers, particularly to men who provided bodies for medical experiments in the nineteenth century. Defective Baptist (the sect the narrator belongs to) seems to have been made up by Mathews—or rather, he gives the name to an old belief, that "not even divine grace can long redeem mortal corruption." Accordingly, "baptism must be renewed at least once a year and each believer must earn his right to the sacrament" (*Tlooth*, 224–25). The narrator, a Defective Baptist, must struggle against "mortal corruption," while Roak, the Fideist, believes her faith (in what?) makes her infallible. Thus the narrator (musician and dental assistant/dentist) seeks revenge for what Roak (doctor) did to her physically. The amputation has ended her career as a violinist and has caused a disease that wracks her body, producing psychological disorder as well (and suggesting a relationship between the narrator and Roak that anticipates the physical/psychological/spiritual confusion and sado-masochism of *Cigarettes*). The narrator's dogged will power (she must *earn* her redemption) flags in Venice but never quite fails until, finally, she comes to acknowledge the power of fate (or chance). Viewed from this perspective, the novel becomes, like the medieval attempts to solve the problem of the hypostatic union, a game that pits the various solutions produced by fate, chance, will, reason, body, and spirit against each other. The fact that prisoners are assigned to sects arbitrarily may invalidate such a reading. Or it may be Mathews's way of suggesting the significance of fate or chance.

## Styles and Digressions

Almost everyone would agree that our view of "reality" is determined to some extent by language. Mathews, according to William McPheron, goes further than this. McPheron points to what he sees as Mathews's "deliberate alignment with that radically skeptical strain of modernism which confines meaning to the temporal play of consciousness within a self-contained universe of verbal signs" (McPheron, 198).[4] Or, put another way, Mathews rejects the modernist attempt to retain the old tradition of metaphor against the rise of relativism that accompanied the revolution in science, philosophy, painting, and music at the beginning of the twentieth century. In life and therefore in literature, Mathews understands "language as an instrument serving not 'to represent [or] show meaning but actually determine it'" (McPheron, 198). It is not surprising, then, that Mathews is the master of various conventional "styles," since those styles have created the way we view certain elements of existence.

Thus, with the escape journey that takes up the second section of the novel, we enter the world of the traditional adventure story, here the mountain trek, complete with strange illnesses, curious natives, savage rituals, tests of endurance. The language is a familiar one:

> To the south, the range we had followed bore eastward, rising to considerable heights. Its peaks were sharp-pointed, or had the form of crenelated towers, with snow-covered platforms at their tops. Clouds perpetually gathered and disintegrated about the summits. . . . Before reaching that colder region, we turned southwest through a pass *perhaps thirty-five thousand feet* high. Soon after, we came on an alpine lake. . . . [I]t contained an abundance of leeches. . . .
>
> The southern slope of the range was warmer and greener. . . . We advanced along a series of easy ridges. Another valley appeared on our right. *Hills of drift-clay and boulders.* . . .
>
> The next ten days were the cruelest. We were kept at difficult altitudes, rarely less than five thousand feet, in freezing or near-freezing weather. Robin's will impelled us through wastes of stone. . . .

Higher still we discovered the remains of an argali, or lum ox—his horns had been caught between the sides of a narrow gorge. The carcass, big as a pony's, was much devoured by birds. (*Tlooth*, 247–48, 279–80)

Passages from the earlier prison camp chapters, in which Mathews uses another traditional style, illustrate his virtuosity:

I had made the ball myself. It was built around two unusual parts—a tiny battery and a pellet of dynamite. From each of the battery's outlets, a wire extended through the hair stuffing of the ball about halfway to the leather wrapper. The free ends of the wires, one of which passed through a firing cap to the dynamite, were six millimeters apart, enough to prevent their junction at a mild impact but not at a sufficiently hard one. The difference, which I had determined exactly, was that between a fast pitch caught and a slow pitch hit. The wire ends separated into meshing sprays of filament, so that no matter how the ball was struck, it was certain to explode. . . .

[The car] was designed on an extravagant scale. The visible machinery was huge—twin pulleys at the front, operated by weighty hand cranks and attached by a web of broad belts to the "rear axle." The hidden machine was an assemblage of bicycles that Beverley had stolen over the years from the Athletic Department. We originally intended to be mounted in tandem, hoping to gain speed by the low resistance of our single file. (*Tlooth*, 188, 224)

This ability of Mathews to shift from one narrative style (and therefore narrative voice) to another makes plausible a narrator growing successively lost in various crises.

The Venice chapters of the novel alternate between actual decadence and the pornographic screenplay being written by the narrator. Naturally, the screenplay mixes elements of Venetian society with erotic fantasy, just as elements of the narrator's life along with fads and fashions of the 1960s (civil rights, rebellion, paramilitarism, etc.) appear, transformed by the fantasy. Finally, the elegantly erotic tour de force culminates in an outrageous funeral:

Bowed in prayer, two black-robed nuns knelt at the head of the bier. At its foot a censer emitted gray smoke in small spurts; and a porcelain box, containing the doctor's viscera, lay beneath the censer. Along the gunnels, candles of some brownish substance burned smokily, unextinguished by the rain.

The gondola was surrounded by eight "mourners," one in front, one behind, three on each side. They swam close to the boat with discreet but impressive power—big crop-headed Negroes, famous in the town (they had come to Venice with the wartime armies and stayed on). Except for a black loincloth, each wore only a fantastic headdress of painted card-board, in the shape of a bishop's miter. Their muscular right arms held aloft links of pine wood, dipped in tarry matter that burned with a dark flame and an abundance of smoke. The smoke was like that of the can-dles in thickness and color—brown streaked with yellow. As they swam the eight men uttered cries of "Wah! Wah!" and from time to time broke into melancholy harmonies:

> "Hear dat moanful soun!
> All de darkies stan a-weepin,
> Massa's in de cole cole groun" (*Tlooth*, 316)

Mathews makes use of an outrageous funeral in *The Conversions* as well, but in this instance the reader doesn't know to what extent one is to take it literally—that is, take it as psychological realism, a delusion of a narrator who suffers from what seems to be syphilis that has resulted in the final loss of identity, a loss begun in the prison camp and intensified during the journey. Or as a fantasy created by the narrator as a part of the novel. Or as a fantasy in which the narrator has become a part of a novel that is now being narrated by someone else. And that, I take it, is the point: we are reading a novel and the erotic dream/nightmare becomes a novel within the novel and that in turn suggests that the first two sections were also novels within a novel: the exhibitions of Canterel in Roussel's *Locus Solus* put in a temporal frame.

Or put another way, the parts of the novel are trap doors dropping the reader through world after world. Section 4, only 23 pages, takes us to four different countries and four different "fictions." The first trap door drops us into India and the fiction of the "exotic native" world of popular books and movies. The narrator, by signing on with medical missionaries, pursues Roak to India, only to discover that she cannot get to Bombay, where Roak is. But we soon forget why the narrator went to India and become caught up in an adventure story, another version of the "census" tale of the opening section. The story involves a natural anesthetic, which saves the narrator and another woman, Nora. While Nora is sleeping under the influence of the anesthetic, her bare feet are seen by a native who believes that bare feet are sacred. He sucks her toes, ingests the anesthetic that is contained in her sweat, and thinks he has experienced the godhead. He brings back friends, who kidnap the narrator and Nora just before a flood comes and kills everyone else. Digression leads to digression, and we are now given a detailed account of how the natives' cattle are saved from the flood because anthills are swept intact onto the plain and the ants aerate and dry out the land before the cattle perish. Nora and the narrator wind up back in the village where they discover that Roak has gone to North Africa, and the narrator, taken in by Carmen, an old friend who just happens to arrive in the village, leaves in pursuit, the trip to India having been as pointless as the escape from the camp and the perilous journey. Pointless, that is, as regards revenge.

The next trap door drops us into Morocco and the "fiction" of a woman who dances herself to death. A cryptic note found by the narrator in Roak's abandoned hotel room begins our fall through another trap door, and we find ourselves in Italy and in a "fiction" similar to that of detective and spy stories of the 1960s in which we are called upon to interpret the narrator's actions in the light of certain "clues," clues which lead us down into a cheese cellar and an encounter with Roak just before the narrator faints. When we awake with the narrator, we find ourselves in a hotel in Savoy where the narrator, the victim or beneficiary of a mysterious conspiracy, is cured of her disease.

In this section of the novel what is most noticeable, other than the frantic pace, is the intensification of the injury, disease, and pain motif. As with all other motifs in the novel, there are "meanings" that we can derive from this one. For example, the suffering of the narrator is but a specific instance of the suffering that pervades the novel from beginning to end, a suffering often treated humorously, if not cynically. Yet the suffering—physical suffering, the pain of the flesh—also results in order and beauty, the novel itself. Thus the grotesque orchestra of the prison camp, in which various parts of human bodies (bones, hair, bladders, etc.) have been turned into musical instruments, can be seen as a metaphor for tragic art, which turns suffering into entertainment. But characteristically, Mathews deflates the tragic, and the grotesque collapses into humor that reaches its climax when a friend, moved by the sounds the orchestra is making, says to the almost weeping narrator, "It is like Beethoven's *Erotica*!" The comic connection of music, sex, and suffering is made in the fourth section when the dancer dances herself to death and when the narrator, on the airplane from Morocco to Rome, endures an excruciating earache until the pain produces "a clearly sounding high A" and culminates in "an oppressive tune that unreeled itself inside my head." ("Unreeled" foreshadows the narrator's being "hooked" by Dr. Cavesenough outside Atri.)

Disease and pain reach their climax in the final scene when the narrator manages to get Roak in a dental chair in France, where, the reader assumes, revenge will be effected. And indeed it is but not through any overt action on the part of the narrator, who, noticing the disease that Roak suffers from, decides simply to let nature take its course.

## The Narrator

Thus *Tlooth*: a novel in which a revenge motif is begun in a footnote, lost over and over again in "styles" and "digressions," and returned to at the end only to dissolve into the description of a print. As was said at the beginning, one could quite honestly describe the work from the outside as a revenge novel of pursuit and suspense; and this description, seen from the inside by the person who has read the novel, would be entirely erroneous.

Seen from the outside—by a novelist or historian or philosopher—life devolves into patterns or into wavelike movements or into cycles or, most popular of all, into intricate cause and effect relationships. Seen from the inside—by the person who leads it—life is a series of events. From time to time we pause and, like an artist or thinker, construct patterns or relationships that may even be "true," but those constructs collapse one after another into the events that follow to become a part of the next search for "meaning." This is not to say that there is no meaning (which, like a belief in meaning, must be grounded in an act of faith), but only that we cannot know that meaning while we are a part of it. "All is human, all divine." In *Tlooth* Mathews confronts the reader with the idea of existence as a search for meaning without conclusion and then further compounds the idea through his selection of narrative voice.

The narrator is, on one level, a puzzle typical of Mathews: we don't realize, until we are far along in the novel, that she is a woman. It's not that Mathews conceals the fact from us; he simply never identifies her sex, and we assume that she is a man. Such an assumption has, we are told these days, deep sociological, political, and psychological implications, but interpreting the novel according to these implications is but another example of prejudiced reading. If, realizing that we have been mistaken, we go back and reconsider—even reread—the novel, then it becomes a different book. What the novel effects is a clever manipulation of *reader response* or *reception* theories of fiction, which locate "meaning" in the reader. In *Tlooth* the "meaning" changes when the person telling the story, not the reader, changes. And at the end, when the narrator falls in love with and marries someone named Joan, the reader begins to wonder if he yet has it right.[5]

In a sense, when it dawns on the reader that the narrator is a woman, he finds himself in a position similar to that of the three surviving escapees from Jacksongrad. While recuperating in a hospital in Kabul, they are visited by a Russian official who informs them that, before they escaped, they had been released—it was to be announced on the day of the escape. Thus the entire desperate journey was unnecessary and pointless, and the second part of the novel, like the first part, dissolves into the narrative itself. Or maybe not. Maybe heroism is heroism regardless of its relevance to any ideal or moral system. And maybe the novel is the novel regardless of who we think is telling it. That a male author would choose a female narrator is, to begin with, an imaginative act that violates psychological, sociological, and political "reality," if one assumes that such reality depends on gender. Just as every attempt to connect the novel to life itself founders on internal contradictions and revelations, so the creator of the novel is an imaginative construct of her opposite. Thus a critic can attack Mathews's "ideas" only by attacking his choice of narrator, and Mathews can counter that attack by pointing out that his novel is obviously, like all art, an imaginative act.

What Mathews has done is "decentered" the novel: that is, while seeming to provide the reader with a center, the narrator, he has actually deprived the reader of a center around which to organize the novel, to shape it into a "unity." The one cause-and-effect relationship that holds the novel together is the narrator's desire for revenge, but in the end the reader is deprived of the violent revenge that he or she (not the narrator) still desires. Yet in a kind of final twist the revenge *is* effected. At the end, when the narrator, still intent on revenge, stares into Roak's mouth and sees the damage her "candy-bomb" has done, she realizes that in fact revenge was effected at the very beginning, when she sent the booby-trapped candy to Roak.

In one sense, then, *Tlooth*, like *The Conversions*, does not end: just as the last riddle is never solved by the narrator, so too we never actually see Roak ruined (and since she shows up in the next novel, we can perhaps say that the revenge is never effected). Moreover, as regards old cause-and-effect realism, it doesn't end because in fact it ended at the very beginning, thus making the novel, from this perspective, pointless.

But on another level *Tlooth*, like *The Conversions*, does have an ending. *Tlooth* opens with the following paragraph: ["Mannish Madame Nevtaya slowly cried 'Fur bowls!' and the Fideist batter, alert to the sense behind the sound of her words, jogged toward first base. The wind from the northern steppe blew coldly on the close of our season" (*Tlooth*, 187)]. Thus the novel begins with a description in words of a game, and it calls attention to "the sense behind the sound of her words." Throughout, the "sense behind the sound" comes and goes elusively. What, for example, is the sense behind the sound of the words in the chapters dealing with eroticism. Mathews imitates a certain kind of erotic writing that is, to begin with, a fantasy. And in *Tlooth* it is doubly a fantasy in that the narrator is making it up as a screenplay for a movie. But all pornography is made up by someone for some popular medium—peep show, movie, book, etc. Pornography is a game but an unsatisfactory game because it arouses emotions that the game itself can't fulfill. The quest for the sense behind the sound can produce only frustration. Of course, what I have just produced is a didactic criticism of this part of the novel. Other criticisms are possible: aesthetic (the writing is not pornographic in that it converts the perverse and sordid into images of grace and beauty); sociological (pornography is a meaningless term since our reactions to words are conditioned by our culture); psychological (the pornography exists in the mind of the narrator and reveals her mental and emotional condition); relativist (i.e., deconstructionist, poststructuralist, postmodern— pornography is in the eye of the reader); Marxist (pornography is the product of a capitalist society); etc.

This section culminates in the narrator's visit to the "oracle." Just before the visit she experiences "contempt for my nature" and believes that "even simple justice was again out of reach." She becomes "indifferent" to what the oracle might tell her. The sound behind the "word" that the oracle pronounces, "Tlooth," can, like the eroticism, the riddles, the reversals, the pointlessness, be interpreted in any number of ways, from its being nothing more than sound, the sound the mud makes as it fills in the hole that her foot made, to "tooth" or "truth" or a combination of the two, to cite only a few possibilities. Yet immediately after the visit to the oracle the narrator says that she "began considering how to pursue my task." The Defective Baptist has been baptized, her indifference is transformed by a "word" into a renewed enthusiasm for revenge, and that enthusiasm in turn leads to more pain and suffering.

So it is only when the narrator comes to see that she accomplished her revenge before she ever left the prison camp, a revenge completed by fate or by whatever games Roak played that carried her to Sfax, that she can say, "I relinquished my opponent to her stars." The sense behind the sound of "her stars," as opposed to "a plenitude of stars" that closes the opening chapter of part 2, must be fate or destiny, and the narration moves outside the temporal order to give us, appropriately, the "picture" of Sfax that closes the novel. The game of the beginning leads to the stasis of the print at the end. The technique, perhaps borrowed from Roussel, goes beyond Roussel's use of it to break down the traditional use of metaphor. Rather the stasis of the painting suggests a connection between time and space. Thus the religious theme, with its emphasis on the problem of the relationship between body and soul, physical and spiritual, a theme echoed in the disease theme, brings the novel to a close, perhaps even in the Fideism of the opening paragraph.

Perhaps. Yet another way to look at the close is to say that it is not a print, it is a description of a print. The sense behind the sound is, metaphorically, outside the temporal altogether—but only metaphorically. At the very end the movement of the novel is captured in the exploding yet motionless fireworks that light up the dark sky. But the picture is a collection of words just as "Fur bowls!" are words spoken within words as Mannish Madame Nevtaya umpires a game that, like a print, can never be reduced to words.

## Chapter Five

# Going Too Far: *The Sinking of the Odradek Stadium*

### The Plot: Treasure Hunts and Con Games

The plot of *The Sinking of the Odradek Stadium* is developed through an exchange of letters between Zachary McCaltex, a librarian living in Miami, and Twang, his Southeast Asian (Pan-Nam) wife, who is in Italy. Twang's letters are written in a very charming and funny broken English that grows more and more accurate as time goes by. They are engaged in research, trying to discover the location of a treasure hidden in the sixteenth century. Twang is in Italy working in libraries there because the treasure was connected with the Medicis; Zachary is examining a collection of sixteenth-entury New World maps because the treasure is thought to have been hidden by a ship's captain (hanged in 1537) and an accomplice somewhere in the Caribbean.

The novel opens midsentence of a letter (". . . confidence in words, Twang"[1]) in which Zachary describes how he has talked with Dexter Hodge, "a very class person whom I have met once before" (*Odradek*, 371). Over a month later he again meets Hodge, who says he has "decided to go into the treasure-hunting racket" and asks Zachary "to join his group" (*Odradek*, 389).

Zachary accepts the invitation, not just to learn the techniques of treasure hunting, as Twang suggests, but because he "would love to move in that world" (*Odradek*, 393). Later Hodge gives him a private tour of the Egyptian Temple, which is described, along with the initiation rite. And Zachary's letters in part 1 conclude with a description of a "baseball game" that Zachary umpires. No paraphrase of this game—which involves a golden box, singing, a disappearing ball, a disappearing Jeep, a six-foot-high cane, the emptying of Zachary's pockets, Hebraic parallelism, and a one-armed pitcher—is possible.

Paralleling this action is what is going on with Twang in Rome and the progress of her research into the whereabouts of the lost treasure. We learn how Zachary and Twang became involved in treasure hunting. On a flight from Rome to Pan-Nam (where he would meet and marry Twang), Zachary met Zonder Tittel. When Zachary told him that he worked in the map section of the Miami University library, Tittel told Zachary of the wreck of a treasure ship in the Florida keys in the sixteenth century. After the wreck two men hid the treasure. One was executed, and the other returned to Italy. It is assumed that "each partner drew a map of the treasure's location" (*Odradek*, 375). Thus Twang is looking for the map in Italy, while Zachary is searching an uncatalogued map collection in Miami.

Part 2 is taken up mainly with two events: Zachary's initiation into a secret organization, the Knights of the Spindle, "the most exclusive club in Florida, with an unvarying membership of sixty-six" (*Odradek*, 411); and Twang's involvement with a man in Florence, where she goes to continue her research into the whereabouts of the treasure. The man, Pindola, attempts to seduce her, goes back to her hotel with her, becomes very drunk, vomits over the railing, and in general makes a fool of himself. "He raise and fall any times on the cobbler stones, he wax eloquence, and he does an aoth on the hat of his mamma he 'll-be ubediant to Twang, and good" (*Odradek*, 415). She tells him that if he will do her a favor she will not have him arrested.

Over a month later Hodge invites Zachary to a house party at the beach. There he types on a "typewriter that is equipped with fully integrated circuits and pigskin keys"; plays poker with Hodge, Peter Jeigh, Roger Taxman, and others; eats "a glorious meal"; and listens to Dr. Clomburger describe "yeast frenzy" and Lester Greek his forthcoming study, *The Confidential Walrus*, in which he establishes "the palindromic precedence of 'Eve' over 'Anna' in *Finnegans Wake*," while Zachary "discoursed on the abstract beauty of maps." He also encounters General Kavya of Pan-Nam. "The one disappointing absence is that of Miles Hood," a legendary figure in Miami (*Odradek*, 446–48).

When Zachary raises the subject of treasure hunting as he and Hodge ride back to town, Hodge will only talk about the legal problems involved. They see Miles Hood walking with his bodyguards, and suddenly someone accosts him and runs off with his attaché case. Hodge pushes Zachary out of the car. "I found myself face to face with the thief. . . . [H]e dropped the case and fled," after which Hodge tells him, "Grab it and we'll split. . . . We'll see Miles later. No point staying and getting our names in the papers" (*Odradek*, 450). But they don't return it. Hodge tells him to keep it until he (Hodge) makes an appointment with Hood.

In Florence, Twang has been working at MAP (the Medici archive), looking for information about the treasure. She has learned why the Medicis could not spend it. Through Pindola she has met Prince Voltic: "he 's trusted with sell of lost heritage of Medici" (*Odradek*, 434). She is also seeing Raymond de Roover, whom she met in Rome. He has been working at MAP for 20 years and knows something about the treasure and about "whawhat happen after 1443" (*Odradek*, 435). Later she meets his wife, Florence de Roover.

Pindola takes her to Prince Voltic's house for drinks, and, seemingly pleased because her knowledge of the Medicis causes him to stop a fruitless search, the Prince sends her a gift. Pindola is pleased because he thinks his association with Twang will get him closer to the Prince. He says he will quit his job as a manicurist. "He 'll kiss under feets of Twang" (*Odradek*, 444).

Pindola tells her that his family have been guardians of some property of the Medici, among which is a chest very like the one that Zachary and Twang are searching for. Thus "my Bonzo [Pindola], he 's be come such an intrestfull chap," and she says she will get as much as she can out of Pindola and the Prince. Accordingly, she plans to go with Pindola and Prince Voltic to a health resort in the mountains.

Part 4 is concerned primarily with Zachary's growing involvement with Miles Hood and his treasure hunting enterprise and with Twang's growing involvement in Italy with Prince Voltic and Pindola and her research into the location of the treasure.

Zachary returns Hood's briefcase, and in return Hood offers him a position in any of his various enterprises: "Radium wells in the mangrove swamps, the dwarf-cattle ranch in the north, treasure-hunting teams— you name it" (*Odradek*, 459). Zachary chooses treasure hunting, but Hood refuses to say exactly what his position will be. As Zachary is leaving Hood's "palace," Hood calls his attention to a statue of a horse, one eye of which is crystal. According to Hood, "'[I]n that glass eye is stored tremendous scrying power.' . . . He peered into the glass eye. 'There's a lady in a sari digging old papers with a spade. I met her once in Rome. A handsome fellow is helping her. I know him too. As a matter of fact, he works for me. Take a gander'" (*Odradek*, 464–65). But Zachary sees nothing and makes no mention of the apparent reference to Twang and Pindola.

The Spindle Knights hold a meeting to discuss plans for the "Miami pre-Lenten Carnival." Zachary is upset because Hood, who is absent, sends word that he (Zachary) is to work with Hodge, who looks at Zachary "as if I were some kind of dogheaded-abortion." But that evening at a party at Dan Tigerbaum's, "Dex was his old affable self, treating me royally" (*Odradek*, 468–69). On his way home from this party Zachary picks a poinsettia blossom and sends it to Twang.

A week later Hood makes Zachary a partner in his treasure hunting enterprise, and Hodge, after being nasty to him, once again reverses himself and offers him "a night on the town." But soon Zachary learns that Hodge has become "Mr. Hood's right hand in the treasure enterprise, and I must have all my dealings with him. I dread that he may try to eliminate me from their plans" (*Odradek*, 477).

During these weeks Twang's involvement with Prince Voltic and Pindola is growing. The Prince employs Pindola to help him "sell off" some Medici goods, and Twang goes to Florence to do research on "a little statue of gold, this the Prince have given Twang to sale. It's of late 15 century" (*Odradek*, 480). And most important to the outcome of the novel, Twang's own research reveals that the last Medici to own the treasure, Silvestro, was in fact the bastard son of Francesco by a slave he bought in 1431, but apparently not a slave from "Black Sea and Alexandria," the usual source.

In part 5 Hood informs Zachary of an April treasure hunting expedition, which might prove very lucrative but which will require a substantial price of admission. At the urging of Twang Zachary agrees to join the expedition and offers to contribute "'certain maps' as part of my stake. . . . Mr. Hood seemed largely, although not entirely, uninterested" (*Odradek*, 486). Otherwise much of Zachary's time is now taken up with the pre-Lenten carnival which is described in some detail.

Twang discovers that their correspondence is being opened and read. She sends Zachary a letter secretly informing him of this fact, tells him that from now on she will write "fake" letters that he is to pay no attention to, and sets up a code by which he will tell her when he wants her to come to Miami for a visit. We are informed in a footnote that this letter, because of insufficient postage, was returned to the sender c/o General Delivery, Florence, and does not get back to Twang for a long time. Thus from this point on Zachary takes Twang's nonsense letters seriously, and Twang believes that Zachary's serious letters are nonsense. And in Zachary's next letter he accidentally uses the code that tells

Twang to come to Miami. The confusion leads to Zachary's going to Italy at the very time that Twang comes to Miami.

Part 6 provides a kind of lull before the furious action of the last part. Zachary learns from Hood that the treasure hunt has been moved up to March, and he will have to come up with his admission fee sooner than expected. Hood also tells him that he saw Hodge in front of Zachary's apartment "talking to a cute little lady in a sari, or whatever it's called in Siam" (*Odradek*, 507). Zachary also has dinner with his sister Diana, who is in Miami on business, and she introduces him to the Asham sisters— Marcia, Molly, and Aline.

Hood tells Zachary that the $2,200 he has raised is not enough, but he agrees to let Zachary use maps he has access to at the library as the remainder of his entrance fee. Dex, who brings this news to him, has "had an intimate dinner with Grace [Odradek] . . . and Grace confided a lot of things that Dex refuses to divulge" (*Odradek*, 514). Zachary finally finds the map he has been looking for, the one that Hood is interested in as well. Twang implies that the map will be useful in her negotiations with the Prince, and Zachary, puzzled, wants to know how she plans to get a copy of it.

Most of Zachary's letters in this section are taken up with descriptions of the Miami Mardi Gras. Meanwhile, in her letters Twang tells him how Silvestro never got his treasure back, was exiled by the Medicis, wandered through Italy and then went with his mother (the ex-slave freed by Silvestro's father) back to her homeland where he became a spice merchant. Twang then requests microfilms of the "baptismals, marriages, deaths records" of the first Italian missionaries who went to Pan-Nam at the end of the fifteenth century (*Odradek*, 511). Zachary sends her the microfilm, wondering what she wants with it.

In part 7 the treasure hunters go to the island indicated on Zachary's map and find the tree marked with a cross, but because the cross is so low on the tree they determine it is a hoax (the implication being that the cross would have grown with the tree over the centuries and would be very high). Back at Hood's office, Hood accuses Hodge of having cheated him. Anything nailed to a tree, he points out, stays where it is nailed. A fight ensues, during which Hodge is shot and presumably killed. Incriminating evidence is destroyed, and Hood tells Zachary to go back to his apartment and stay out of sight.

Zachary's mother dies, and, accompanied by Hood, he attends her funeral. He then discovers that Hodge is still alive, and soon thereafter three of Hood's bodyguards appear at his door, tell him the partnership is dissolved, and warn him to forget about Hodge, who was not actually murdered. Finally, Hood disappears.

Meanwhile in Italy the police search Twang's room. She discovers that they were sent by the American Mr. P. Asher, ostensibly because a cameo she and Prince Voltic sold him was a fake. Voltic assures her he will do what he can for her, and later he tells her that he will take responsibility for the cameo. She turns over to the Prince the "Medici papers, map and explanations" (*Odradek*, 537), and she and Pindola escape to Lerici. For a reason Zachary cannot figure out, Twang tells him that, though her map and his map match, it doesn't matter because the treasure belongs to Prince Voltic. But, "not a matter anynow" (*Odradek*, 535).

It is apparent that Zachary has been the victim of an elaborate confidence game, played on him by Hood, Hodge, Voltic, and the others in an attempt to get a treasure map that he has access to. But because of the confusion caused by the undelivered letter, he sees Twang as a part of, rather than a victim of, the swindle. Confronted with what seems to him to be betrayal on both sides of the Atlantic, he writes Twang, accusing her of having been in on the con from the very beginning. And in his next (and final letter) he makes essentially the same accusation, but this time in the jargon of the con man. What follows is the complete text of his final letter:

> This chump never blowed you were turned out to hopscotch. You let him find the leather and he copped you for the pure quill, when you're nothing but a crow. It took a long time to bobble him but now you've knocked him good and he feels like a heavy gee had slipped him a shiv. Well, no twist will ever beat this savage again, not if she hands over her bottom bumblebee—it's cheaper loaning cush to Pogy O'Brien. Don't you play the hinge but stick to the big con. You're a class raggle with a grand future, even if this mark knows you're snider. (*Odradek*, 544)

Twang, in her final letters, writes first to de Roover, explaining to him that the treasure never in fact left Italy. She then writes Zachary, explaining that her crucial letter was never delivered and so they have been at cross-purposes ever since. And at last the significance of the enigmatic title of the novel becomes apparent. She explains how she secured the treasure from Pindola (without his knowing it, of course) and got it to Genoa, where she had it loaded on "the *Odradek Stadion*. . . . It will carry the box to Rangoon, best market of gold in this material-subtle world" (*Odradek*, 552). She has not, however, been able to insure it.

The rest of the letter contains a beautiful expression of her love for and devotion to Zachary. Whether the letter is complete we don't know since there is no period at the end of it. And more important, we don't know whether Zachary ever received the letter, let alone believed it: "I have telephoned but it will not answer, and shall wire but you will not believe it . . ." (*Odradek*, 554).

## Mysteries and Enigmas

The end raises a problem that has underlain the story from the beginning: who is the editor of the letters and how did he secure them? It is apparent that *Odradek* is a fragment retrieved from a larger document, retrieved somewhat violently, it would seem, since it opens and possibly closes with incomplete sentences. But the reader easily forgets, as he moves through the work, that it is a fragment. As we have seen, something similar is true of *The Conversions*. While not obviously a fragment, it must finally be viewed in the light of a wider reality, a reality that remains enigmatic. In *Odradek* that wider reality is established right from the beginning and carried so subtly past the end that at least one critic has failed to notice the absence of a period (Mottram, 171).[2] So the first question to ask when one begins analyzing the novel is, Whose document is it? That is, who is working with it, has edited it and added the appendix? But of course this is not the first question that readers ask, just as we don't ask when we set out to put it together who created a jigsaw puzzle and for what purpose. In fact, beginning midsentence paradoxically ensures the involvement of the readers by telling them that something *is* left out, that there is a mystery to solve.

There are a number of mysteries to solve. For example, how did a librarian in Miami come to marry a woman from Indochina (Pan-Nam) and why is she now in Italy? Why should these two people be trying to find a treasure? These are relatively easy enigmas, resolved within the text itself. The nature of the treasure is more difficult. As we will see, it constitutes one of the two main "plots." Paralleling the mystery of the treasure are the natures of the individuals in Miami, Rome, and Florence whom Zachary and Twang become involved with. This mystery, running beside the mystery of the treasure, is solved, probably somewhat before the end by most readers. And there is another mystery, adumbrated in subtle ways—the mystery of Twang's ancestry, which very few readers will even know about until it is solved.

There are two main plots: that concerning Zachary and Twang, developed through an exchange of letters; and that concerning a treasure and its whereabouts from the fourteenth century on, developed within the correspondence. This latter plot involves the Holy City of Christendom, Rome, while the former involves the Holy City of contemporary America, Miami. The actual time consumed by the novel is a little over a year (April 1 or 2—April Fools Day? Easter?—to April 13, Holy Saturday, of the following year), but through flashbacks developed by the letters we discover how Zachary learned about the treasure, how he met and married Twang, and how they came to be in Italy and the United States.

The gradual unfolding of the treasure search is paralleled by the gradual improvement of Twang's English as she writes letter after letter and by the gradual revelation of a confidence game being played on Zachary and Twang. The common denominator here is language: Twang's pidgin English and Zachary's underworld slang, a parallel hinted at in humorous references to semiotics and language theory (*Odradek*, 390–91). At the end Twang's English is on the verge of being what most would consider fluent, while Zachary's last letter is written entirely in the argot of the confidence man. Much of the fascination of the novel lies in these games it plays with the reader, games enhanced by an index which seems to be eccentric and incomplete (and perhaps inaccurate). I say "seems" because the work it indexes is a fragment. But the index establishes that the work we have has been saved for other than aesthetic reasons.

## The Limits of Modernism

To read the novel this way is to read it as a work in the tradition of Realism. Its form—the epistolary novel—is certainly in that tradition. And its use of patterns of allusion, imagery, and possibly symbolism along with its shifting perspectives makes it very much a part of the modernist manipulation of Realism. Thus the novel opens with an allusion to language, " . . . confidence in words"; the first letter, in its mention of cow and cat and lamb and eagle owl, begins the animal imagery that pervades the novel; and its references to Santiago de Compostella, cherubs, and Good Friday establish the religious theme. As in a musical composition, these themes, once established, are used throughout to support the main theme, the plot, Zachary's and Twang's search for the treasure. The themes often come together, as in—to cite a minor example—the word *crow*, which signifies not only the animal but also, in

underworld slang, a phony. And crows are what are thought to embell-
ish the chest that contains the treasure. That this is a mistake connects
crows, as we will see, to yet another theme in the novel. At other times
the themes are set in counterpoint. Thus Dharmabody, Zachary's dog,
whose name never appears in the index and must be found under the
general heading "dog," represents Zachary's loyalty and devotion, and
when Twang refers to the dog in her last letter, she ironically points up
Zachary's failure. As a more complete and ambiguous example of the
interweaving of imagery and allusion, consider the description of the initiation Zachary must undergo to become a Knight of the Spindle.

First, there is the preparation for initiation during which Zachary is
fitted for his robes: "purple-red cloth, worked with random crescents of
silver" (*Odradek*, 416). While this is being done, Zachary, with Hodge's
help, picks the "truest" of three pictures (one of which contains a triangle) and justifies his choice. Passing this test (with Hodge's help), he goes
from the tailor's shop to a one-horse carriage, which takes him on a long
ride and a turn "around a colossal manhole, the principal entrance to the
Dade County sewer complex" (*Odradek*, 417).

For his next test he is taken out to sea on a fishing boat. "I noticed,
near the dallying boat, an effect as of floating cloth-of-gold." When he
asks what it is, the captain grins and points to an examiner who is
arranging metal filings "in half-inch mounds: almost touching one
another, they formed a closed, irregular curve." The vibration of the
engine shakes the filings "into a fixed equilateral triangle." The examiner then asks two questions, which Zachary, to his surprise, answers cor-
rectly and without hesitation.

> "Can you define what you see?"
> "A triangle is defined by its center—its unmanifest essence."
> "Is this to be explained?"
> "No, only sensed in its intensity."

Looking back, Zachary sees the other persons on the boat, and behind
the boat "the cloth-of-gold was now in focus: loose-stemmed water-
weeds." When he asks why both this test and the one at the tailor's
shop contained a triangle, the examiner says that it was not deliberate,
explains the second triangle, and says, "'Chance is a wise master'"
(*Odradek*, 419–20).

On the way home he is once again put into the one-horse carriage,
and the examiner hands him "a morocco pouch with one gold coin in

it—an *écu sans soleil*." A long ride takes him twice by the manhole, and
Zachary has "become convinced that in my dealings with the Knights
everything that happens is symbolic" (*Odradek*, 420).

Almost two weeks later the Knights come for Zachary, take him back
to the manhole, blindfold him, lead him down into the sewers beneath
the city, put him in a boat, remove the blindfold, and warn him not to
look back ("don't play the hinge"). There follows a boat ride between
walls that blaze with changing light, while the "smell remained con-
stant" and irritated shouts and enigmatic phrases "moaned away down
the galleries amid a salad of colors." At the end of the ride a platform
rises from the water. On it are several dozen men seated in armchairs,
among them Dexter Hodge, Miles Hood, and Robert Pindola. Zachary
is given an armchair, the men sing the opening of the Spindle Hymn,
and "four Knights delivered brief speeches on 'aspects of Spindledom'"
(*Odradek*, 421–24).

The mayor of Miami is the next speaker. He gives an account of
Spindle Knight Roger Taxman's battle in the Sahara to save a chained
maiden from the Great Sand Snake. "[H]e stuck it through the eye with
the hole-punching blade of his Swiss Army knife, then finished him off
in the customary manner" (*Odradek*, 426).

The mayor welcomes Zachary as a new Spindle Knight, says to him,
"'That's two hundred and ninety-eight dollars,'" and gives him a pad of
blank checks so that he can pay the initiation fee. A curtain behind the
podium rises, revealing "the workshop of the Knights, where their pre-
cious Galahad linen was made. A token crew now worked its cumbrous
machines." Zachary is shown the stages of linen manufacture, at the end
of which the spinster "tapped me on either shoulder with the spindle,
saying, 'Theah . . . and theah . . . I pronounces you a Knight of the
Thimble'" (*Odradek*, 427–29).

Zachary ascends a ladder and high above the others reads "from
Petrarch's description of Mont Ventoux; Hannibal splitting the Alps
with vinegar was crossed out" (*Odradek*, 429). While he reads, the
Knights file out singing what is apparently the last verse of the Spindle
Hymn. He follows them into an adjoining room where they eat and
drink and enjoy themselves until dawn.

Such description may be Mathews's manipulation of the modernist
tradition, his removal of the remnant of representation that it retained.
To what extent he is also parodying it, if he parodies it at all, is hard to
say. Certainly the references to *The Waste Land* in the novel are meant to
be humorous (*Odradek*, 450, 452, 454). Perhaps only the humor is

extended in the description of the thugs fishing off the back of the boat in the Everglades (*Odradek*, 529), or perhaps readers are so conditioned to look for "meaning" in everything that they find it in everything, even in men fishing in the Everglades. Or perhaps Mathews, knowing the prejudices of his readers, purposely misleads them. Or perhaps he does both: uses *The Waste Land* to point up his own "Unreal City," Miami, while he makes fun of the allusion.

## Characterization

Whatever Mathews's intentions may be, *Odradek*, more than *The Conversions* and *Tlooth*, grounds its games in human emotion. Where the narrator of *The Conversions* is motivated by vague and uncertain emotions and the narrator of *Tlooth* is driven by a desire for revenge that is stated but never fully developed, in *Odradek* love and loyalty pervade the novel from Zachary's opening expression of desire to Twang's final plea for understanding and acceptance. On this level *Odradek* is a novel of love tested by lust and greed. Consequently, character is of the utmost importance.

Twang's character is consistent and plausible. She is obviously the more intelligent and more emotionally stable of the two. The novel, I think, leaves no doubt that she is faithful to Zachary, and one of the most moving elements of the story is her devotion to him, even as she is sometimes as amused by his foibles as the reader. Of course, much of the humor lies in her attempt to come to grips with the traps and pitfalls of the English language and her attempt—tiny Oriental that she is—to deal with the con men who assault her. But Mathews never allows her to fall into the stereotype of either the Oriental or the Little Woman. Moreover, her character makes it plain that the characterizations of the first two novels were matters of choice, not weakness or uncertainty.

Zachary is no less a triumph, but he raises problems. It's not surprising, considering the character of Zachary and the inclusion of an index, that critics have found the novel Nabokovian.[3] Both authors exhibit a playfulness that grows from their wonderful mastery of language. Yet in this novel, because it is so much a novel of character, the mysteries of Zachary's thoughts and actions—and in particular his language—go beyond the playfulness of a game that justifies similar traits in *Tlooth* (and in *Pale Fire*). Why, for example, should a university librarian be familiar with the argot of confidence men? Is his familiarity genuine? If so, is he a con man, and if he is, is he conning Twang? Obviously not, and in fact his use of argot appears forced, as though he's playing a role (but of course confidence games are based on role playing). Yet since there is no marked increase in Zachary's use of slang up to the final letter, the novel doesn't seem to use it to record a descent into corruption.

He seems at times to be pretending to be the con man, using the argot self-consciously. Thus he sets off "find the leather" in quotation marks and of "blowing the chase" remarks "whatever that means."[4] Yet his first use of the argot of the con artist, when he describes himself as feeling "like a beaten mark" in the first letter, is so natural as to be overlooked by the reader; and even "cop a heel," which he uses in his second letter, seems spontaneous enough. At best his use of the argot is ambiguous. One could cite his knowledge of "Carrie Watson" and "Pogy O'Brien" as proof either that he is very familiar with the confidence world or that he is obviously an outsider overusing a language he doesn't really "feel." The problem is compounded by the fragmentary nature of the work. There are numerous allusions to events that occurred earlier, some well developed (e.g., his trip to Pan-Nam and marriage to Twang). But others are more obscure, especially his relationship with Dan and Grace, whose last name, we learn from the index, is Odradek and with whom he seems to have had an affair (*Odradek*, 433). Even his final letter can be interpreted either as a revelation of what he has been throughout or as evidence of his disintegration.

Most readers will find Zachary an engaging character, by turns witty and naive and charming and ludicrous and likeable and grotesque. In this reading the letters "C" and "CI" are the climax of the novel: Twang's letter, written in her native language, represents her triumph, her preservation of her integrity against the onslaught of greed and seeming betrayal—she preserves her own language while mastering another; "CI," Zachary's last letter (quoted earlier), written in slang, represents his failure, his collapse into pitiful role playing—there is no further letter from him so his old voice never reappears.

But in order to read *The Sinking of the Odradek Stadium* as simply a Realistic or even a modernist novel in the received meaning of that term, the reader must not only overlook much description: a world in which China is about to bomb Mars, in which the United States has 51 states, in which the city of Miami stages a huge Mardi Gras celebration and contains citizens who roast "seven lambs" on "a steam-powered spit," a world of watchcats and secret organizations of con men, etc.; he must also overlook the fact that characterization often becomes bizarre, if not fantastic. Consider, for example, Dexter Hodge, known as "the invisible Jesuit":

> [He contributes] to civic projects, advancing the cause of urban planning, and providing directly or indirectly many jobs in the Greater Miami area. He attends concerts and lectures, is a director of our Revival of Reading chapter, and from time to time publishes a sonnet in *Sewanee Review*. . . . Every afternoon he visits his friend Silex Jewcett, who has spent half his long life in prison but is revered by the people of Florida as a saint. Hodge arrives at the municipal jail with a chamber band of thirteen sarrusophones playing spirituals . . . and leaves to the invariable strains of "Praise God from Whom all blessings flow." . . . [H]e is a great sportsman . . . has sponsored several swift milers, his *sepak raga* team . . . boasts the fastest elbows in the West, and he is the source, guide and goalie of the soccer team. (*Odradek*, 392–93)

He directs "the Egyptian Temple, a 'psychic gymnasium' whose activities are secret. Its members undergo an initiation that includes some form of baptism" (*Odradek*, 392). He is "responsible [for] the New Wars Shrine . . . built entirely out of weapons," while his "own house . . . is a jewel of classic modern. It is built in the shape of a sundial. . . . Its one stark ornament is a high relief over the front door representing two wolves seated face to face, and between them a slender candle burning with a perpetual gas flame" (*Odradek*, 393).

And when Zachary goes into "the bowels of [Hood's] palace" he finds

> Mr. Hood in a windowless room whose walls were hung with old lutes. He was swinging in a deep hammock, concealed except for one tiny protruding hand, which beat time to a ditty that a young man, on a nearby stool, sang to the plunking of a mandoline:
>
> A fine rain anoints the canal machinery. . . .
>
> . . . He then took me by the arm, and with a silent, expansive gesture invited me to admire the splendors about us.
> This began a tour of Mr. Hood's indoor domain, or at least that part of it devoted to scholarship. We visited a room where students were repairing prints of old movies, among them an early lost Laurel; another where three ham sets busily whined—one operator announced excitedly, "I've got the Dahomey *Die Schwärmer!*"; a third where a battery of computers blinked away at translations of middle Bactrian; and at last the immense library, where many young people were at work. Mr. Hood explained their tasks as we circled the room. ". . . clear text of

Boethius . . . fodder for my theoretical teas . . . Chomskian refutations . . .
Here is the star of the show. (*Odradek*, 463)

The "star of the show" is "a blonde girl, who bore an uncanny resemblance to Hyperion Scarparo [the right fielder of the Cannon baseball
team], 'rehearsing Mommsen.'" Hood says, "Every day she reads to me
from the classics of history. It is an *heure sacrée*" (*Odradek*, 464).

## Puzzles, Play, and Ritual

The fantastic elements in the plot, however, are vitally related to the
realism in that they render plausible certain metaphoric or symbolic
associations. Late in the novel Zachary writes, "When I was twelve, my
parents brought us up here [to Miami] for Easter, and they lost me when
they started home" (*Odradek*, 498). The statement surprises the reader
because the characters in Mathews's early novels almost never reminisce
about their childhoods or their ancestry. We know nothing and practically nothing about the pasts of the narrators of *The Conversions* and
*Tlooth*. In fact, in the first two novels Mathews only rarely uses even
flashbacks, and when he does he only hints at events from a past that
remains enigmatic. Since we know nothing of their parents, homes,
schools, family, we don't know what role, if any, those people and places
and institutions played in the formation of the man and woman who tell
us their stories. Obviously, Mathews makes use of a technique outside
the bounds of conventional Realism. And Mathews's narrators are not
quite like Marlow in Conrad's fiction (to cite one of the best known
examples from the modernist period), for though Marlow has no past,
very little existence outside the story he tells, his voice, manner, and
actions all establish him as the typical Englishman in attitudes and values. That, after all, is the point. He provides what is perhaps Conrad's
judgment but without that judgment's omniscient authority. The narrators of *The Conversions* and *Tlooth* are atypical, representative of no established moralities or worldviews. More like Flann O'Brien's John
Furriskey in *At Swim-Two-Birds* who "was born at the age of twenty-five
and entered the world with a memory but without personal experience
to account for it,"[5] their surfaces are there before us; we can only specu-
late as to what created those surfaces.

Or, to use his own characterization borrowed from Georges Perec,
Mathews plunges us into a jigsaw puzzle. Perec develops "the art of
jigsaw puzzling" (by which he means "wooden puzzles cut by hand" as

opposed to machine-made "arbitrary" puzzles) in the preamble to *Life A User's Manual*.[6] "The pieces [of a jigsaw puzzle] are readable, take on a sense, only when assembled; in isolation, a puzzle piece means nothing" (Perec, [xiii]). Mathews turns the reader into a jigsaw puzzle solver, but as Perec points out, "[d]espite appearances, puzzling is not a solitary game: every move the puzzler makes, the puzzle-maker has made before . . . every blunder and every insight, each hope and each discouragement have all been designed, calculated, and decided by the other" (Perec, [xv]). Certainly such a description fits *The Conversions* and *Tlooth* in which "the organized, coherent, structured signifying space of the picture is cut up not only into inert, formless elements containing little information or signifying power, but also into falsified elements, carrying false information" (Perec, [xv]). One must substitute "story" for "picture" but such a substitution is precisely the point: like Roussel in *Locus Solus*, Mathews flattens time (cause and effect), suggesting a reality that is spatial rather than temporal. In this respect Mathews achieves unity, the unity of a game. The game played between Wayl and the narrator in *The Conversions*, like the game played between the narrator and Roak in *Tlooth*, becomes a part of the game played between Mathews and the reader. And in these early novels Mathews seems obsessed with not letting the reader forget that it is a game. Or, to quote him: "I certainly intend to make it as difficult as possible for any reader not to realize that the experience he is having is that of reading (rather than an experience of what the written words are describing or representing); this seems a useful thing to do, since it corresponds to what is in fact happening and constitutes a truly realistic element in what I write" (Interview).

When Mathews says, "Representation ('realism') and 'self expression' strike me as much more dubious points of departure" than "[m]aking a game of inventing the plot" (Interview), he reminds us of those who think that the contemporary writer must "invent" (as opposed to "find") a common ground with the audience. The justification seems to be honesty (i.e., "the experience [the reader] is having is that of reading" rather than of life itself). The notion that the reader must be made to realize that art is not life is a subtle version of the age-old attempt by artists to demolish the barrier between artist and audience. According to Mathews, since the reader is "reading" and not "experiencing" reality, making him or her aware of what is being done "corresponds to what is in fact happening and constitutes a truly realistic element in what I write" (Interview).

"Truly" suggests that Mathews's insistence that his fiction is not "realistic" is, in fact, more realistic than the illusion he creates in his fiction. Plot cannot imitate life; at best it can imitate an action, but that action must be given a beginning and an end. Thus "plot has an inevitably 'abstract' element in it that must be attended to independently of everything else." Plot becomes a game played between writer and reader, and "in what games does communication not take place, all the time and often at a high pitch of intensity?" As an example Mathews cites tennis: "Lendl and Becker face to face, and . . . the people watching them" (Interview). But what is communicated during a tennis match? And does it transcend the game itself? Is the act of reading comparable, even loosely, to watching or participating in a game?

The answer depends upon what one means by "reading." Mathews says that the experience of reading is not "the experience the written words are describing or representing," an assertion one cannot argue with. But he also says, "I'd be happy to think that my written language somehow visibly disclaims any justification by subject or external reference: all values of thought, feeling, and imagination are created entirely by the reader using the materials I supply on the page" (Interview). If "materials" includes plot along with characterization, imagery, metaphor, and all the other elements of fiction, then Mathews only appears to give the job of creation to the reader since it is hard to see how values that depend upon such material are "created *entirely* by the reader." As Perec points out, "[E]very move the puzzler makes, the puzzle-maker has made before" (Perec, [xv]).

Yet the first two novels undeniably have the quality of invention that Mathews refers to, so much so that character seems to exist for the purpose of plot, not in the Aristotelian sense that only through action can character be realized, but in the way that the nature of a game ultimately determines the nature of the people who master it. *The Conversions* and *Tlooth* are made up of pieces that "are readable only when assembled," are works in which "the pattern determines the parts." Mathews says that the "two or three remarks" the narrator of *The Conversions* makes about himself are "enough to suggest all the things that he's not saying that he should be saying" (Tillman, 34), but for most readers he remains the man who plays the game and loses . . . perhaps. The narrator of *Tlooth* is a bit more fully developed and evokes sympathy mainly because of her physical suffering, but the reader needs more than the "materials" Mathews supplies to make her fully three dimensional. In the early novels the games he plays with his readers tend to be more competitive than cooperative.[7]

But, though play dominates both novels, there is a shift in emphasis, a shift that continues in *The Sinking of the Odradek Stadium* to the point that character comes to compete with plot. By the time Zachary recalls his childhood trip to Miami we already know far more about him than we knew about the narrators of the first two novels, and the sudden intrusion of the reminiscence serves to remind us of just how much we do know. And also of how most of what we know operates on two or more levels, for after telling us of his childhood journey, Zachary goes on to say, "[A]nd they lost me when they started home. . . . I was then punished for hiding myself deliberately, which I had not done. Miami became a place of doom" (*Odradek*, 498). The parallel is obvious, not only as regards the Miami that Mathews creates, a city that stages a fantastic Mardi Gras festival, but as regards the season of Lent, which takes place during the last section of the novel and closes with a letter written on the afternoon or evening of Holy Saturday, a letter that may or may not reach the person to whom it is sent.

The novel opens at the "end of Lent" when Zachary, having been reduced to a "beaten mark" (*Odradek*, 368) on Good Friday, beholds in a new hotel, "the Brissy St. Jouin . . . the 'Naples ultra' of Miami splendor," a modern cross: "Above the lobby fountain, seven [television] sets rose vertically from a spray-shrouded base. On either side of the midmost screen, three others were horizontally aligned, hung by transparent cords from the distant ceiling" (*Odradek*, 365). In this "monument to intercontinental awareness" Zachary ironically beholds what will be his true cross, his ultimate lack of "intercontinental awareness" during Easter of the next year. The Christian metaphor is interwoven with others: *The Waste Land* suggests the decay of the old mystery cults and connects with Twang's Zen stories; that Zachary's sister is named Diana reinforces the pervasive use of mythology. All these metaphors culminate in the Mardi Gras celebration with its eclectic mixture of everything from the mysterious "Guest" to the dog race through Miami: at once an update of the modernist obsession with alienation and a wildly humorous treatment of it.

This is not to say that *Odradek* is Mathews's version of *The Waste Land*. The novel contains no detached moral voice or vision, and whoever has retrieved the document for whatever reason never makes a moral pronouncement. At the heart of all the images and metaphors and intricate games lies the relationship between Twang and Zachary, and Mathews, by implication, has a great deal of sympathy for both. In a sense this is a crucial difference not only between Mathews and Nabokov but also between Mathews and the Thomas Pynchon of *The Crying of Lot 49*. There are obvious similarities between the two novels, beginning with the titles, the meaning of each becoming clear only at the end, but, finally, Mathews's work is simultaneously more aesthetically detached and more emotionally involved. In my view Mathews's "religious devotion" to language transcends the bounds of game playing, for in a game "communication" cannot transcend the game itself. If it does, game becomes ritual.

## Closure

Nor is this to say that the novel, to the very end, doesn't remain elusive. It does, just as *The Conversions* and *Tlooth* do. After all, the novel is about lies and deception and turns on a mistake, a letter that doesn't reach its destination. Both treasure hunts (Medici and modern) contain false leads and clues that go nowhere. Anything seems to be possible, from a straight-out realistic reading to the nihilism of certain linguistic theories suggested by the conversation that Twang overhears and can't understand (*Odradek*, 390–91).

The opening of the novel, in addition to everything else that it does, also sets up this theme of the mistake, both obviously—"*batrimoine*" for "*patrimoine*"—and more subtly—the horizontal rank of television sets does not cross, as Zachary says it does, at the "midmost" point of the vertical rank but just above the middle, which makes it more a cross in the Christian sense (*Odradek*, 365–67). Thus the reader, if he or she catches this mistake, is forewarned: in a Mathews novel—and particularly in a Mathews novel about the big con—no one is safe.

The plot is concluded through Twang's final letter, written in an English that signifies her conquest of more than language, which reveals (1) that a letter that never reached its destination has caused great confusion; (2) that the treasure never left Italy; (3) that Twang is the rightful heir to the treasure; (4) that the treasure has been secured and loaded for shipment to Burma on a ship called the *Odradek Stadion*. Thus the "game" set up in the opening letter is over.

But this game, like all games, exists in a wider context, and what needs to be determined is whether it moves outside itself and becomes ritual. First, there are mysteries within the game that are not resolved.

What does the Greek "Stadion" as opposed to the Latin "Stadium" signify (if anything)? What has Grace Odradek to do with the Odradek Stadium/Stadion (if anything or maybe the index is wrong)? Were Dan and Grace in collusion against (or with) Zachary, and if so, what is the motive (that Zachary spurned Grace for Twang [*Odradek*, 412])? Does the Odradek Stadium actually contain the treasure (see *Cigarettes*)? And does Zachary receive the final letter?

These last two questions take us to the second level of "context." Who has retrieved the fragment and for what purpose? One possibility—the most likely one, I suppose—is that what we have is a document in yet another treasure hunt by someone trying to find the treasure. That treasure hunt may be a dead end, or the hunter may be able to get to or raise the ship now that he knows it contains the treasure or, as indicated earlier, he may have discovered some connection between Grace and Dan and may know that the treasure didn't go down with the ship. Or, most unlikely but possible, Zachary has been conning Twang and has disappeared because he, through Grace and Dan, has secured the treasure. At the end he may be the ace con man blowing the mark, but, again as indicated earlier, his role in the con is at best highly ambiguous. It is even possible that Mathews has given us, somewhere along the way, the answer to all these questions (e.g., the quotation from Kafka at the beginning may be the key to Zachary). One thing is certain: not all questions are answered by the title of the novel any more than solving the final riddle in *The Conversions* answers all the questions in that novel. In fact, the title, *The Sinking of the Odradek Stadium*, is, like everything else in the novel, successful on a number of levels.

First, of course, it is the "end" of the plot contained in the title, the significance of which does not become apparent until the end—a game that turns on the ultimate irony of structure. In this it is similar to the revelation of the race of the narrator in *The Conversions* and the sex of the narrator in *Tlooth*. But just as in those works, it turns us back into the novel once again and forces us to view all the games, con and otherwise, in a new light. The temptation is to claim that our understanding is determined by the text, that we can't go outside it, but paradoxically, since the text is fragmentary, such a critical position forces us outside the text. Thus Mathews's stated method, "[A]ll values of thought, feeling, and imagination are created entirely by the reader using the materials I supply on the page," both limits the imagination of the reader and at the

same time frees the imagination. As in the previous novels, the reader
participates in the construction of the fiction and in so doing moves the
fiction into the realm of "real life"—or moves real life into the realm of
"fiction."

# Chapter Six
# Going Back: *Cigarettes*

## Structure and Point of View

*Cigarettes* is, on one level, a novel of manners that has been compared with the fiction of Jane Austen.[1] It deals with a certain narrow class—roughly the upper-middle-class society of upstate New York and New York City, people involved in business, horse racing and the art world, primarily but not exclusively WASP. The locations—New York City, Saratoga Springs, Albany, etc.—are described realistically, and the characters are developed through cause-and-effect relationships, some beginning in childhood. But the comparison with Austen gives the person unfamiliar with the book a very misleading impression. Something of the same thing is true, as we have seen, of Mathews's other novels. *The Conversions* could be called a detective or mystery story; *Tlooth* is cast within the framework of a chase or adventure novel; and *The Sinking of the Odradek Stadium* is on one level an epistolary novel. By altering the time sequence and alluding to events and people that are left undeveloped, Mathews transforms a realistic narrative into an intriguing experiment. Mathews himself, in speaking of *Cigarettes*, remarks: "It started as an attempt to solve a specific problem . . . how to tell a story about a group of people belonging to the New York art and business world in a way that would allow the reader to make it up" (Ash, 31).

Most of the action takes place during two time periods—1936–38 and 1962–63—with almost 80 percent of the novel given over to the latter period. There are two chapters, 25 pages in all, that bridge the two periods, and one that covers in 11 pages the period from 1945 to 1963. And in the chapters devoted to 1962–63 there are references to the earlier period and vice versa. But for the most part the prewar and postwar actions stand independent of each other as regards any narrative chain of cause and effect. This is not to say that there is no causality but only that if it exists, it must be derived mainly from the juxtaposition of the two periods. I will return to this point.

What does connect the two periods is the portrait of Elizabeth, painted in 1936 and copied, stolen, bought, sold, and seemingly (but not actually) destroyed during 1961–63. It is important in several ways: its subject is central to the novel's concern with sexuality and love; it is painted by Walter Trale, who originally specialized in the painting of animals, racehorses mainly; and because it becomes a valuable "object," it has to be insured by its wealthy owners. Thus it brings together the three "worlds" of the novel—art, racing, and finance—as well as the two locations, New York City and upstate New York, that also join the two periods. Yet the subject of the painting is, among the main characters, the person that we know least about as regards heredity and environment, and we are told practically nothing about the painting except that it doesn't look like Elizabeth.[2] At the end Phoebe, who is still young (21) and Elizabeth, who is middle aged (approximately 50 or 51) both die. Phoebe's copy of the portrait hangs on the wall of her hospital room; the original hangs in the house where Elizabeth—the true "original," as she calls herself (*Cigarettes*, 253), who was about 24 or 25 when it was painted—dies.

It is perhaps important to note that World War II, which must have been a crucial event in the lives of both the older characters, all of whom were born between 1910 and 1920, and the younger characters, all of whom, with the exception of Irene, were born during the war, is referred to only in passing.[3] But often in Mathews's fiction what isn't there is as important as what is; and perhaps it is significant that the two periods are both prewar.

There is, as always in Mathews's fiction, the question of point of view as it relates to unity and to cause and effect. Though the novel begins and ends with Lewis Lewison as narrator, it is not a conventional "first-person" narrative. It is, in fact, point of view that, once again, first forces a rereading of the novel.

I have first discussed the nature of the connections between the two periods to emphasize that, though *Cigarettes* begins and ends in the summer and early fall of 1963, it is by no means a conventional flashback novel. Nor does it attempt to impose a spurious circular structure on disparate events. On the other hand, such a circular structure is available to readers if they want to use it to "make it up."

## A Tapestry of Stories

The novel opens with an account of a brief affair between Allan Ludlam and Elizabeth (only a part of her last name, "Hea-," is ever given) in July 1963 in a resort town in upstate New York. The relationship ends abruptly, and Allan discovers that his wife, Maud, knows about the affair and that Elizabeth is living with his wife.

The action then shifts to the summer of 1936 in the same resort town and to another affair, this one between Elizabeth and Oliver Pruell, a man 22 years old, two or three years younger than herself. Their affair comes to an end when she abandons him for an afternoon, meets Walter Trale, a young man (approximately 18 years old), who has already established a reputation as a painter of racehorses, and offers to pose for a portrait. Oliver leaves the resort town for New York City to begin his career in business.

There follows an account of the relationship between Oliver and Pauline Dunlap, the younger sister of Maud, in the summer of 1938. Most of the Dunlap fortune (not nearly as large as people outside the family think) has been left to Maud, but the sisters agree to let it be thought that they share equally in it in order to make Pauline more "eligible." Pauline pursues Oliver until he gives in, they begin an affair, and, believing that she is richer than she actually is, he marries her.

To this point characters and location provide definite links between events, and Mathews seems to be developing a chain that will lead back to Allan and Elizabeth in 1963. But the next section abruptly introduces two characters, Owen Lewison and his daughter Phoebe, who seem to be in no way connected with what has gone before except by coincidence: "Years later, on the very July first that Allan Ludlam discovered Elizabeth, and in the same town, Owen Lewison instructed his bank in the city to settle a large sum of money on his daughter, Phoebe, then on the eve of her twenty-first birthday" (*Cigarettes*, 42). After this, readers will be provided with action, conversations, and events—facts, if you like—but Mathews will make very few connections; the reader will have to invent or at least construct the "plot."

The period 1961–63 involves the following "stories":

(1) Owen and Phoebe. Owen settles money on his daughter Phoebe, then takes it away from her when she refuses to let him control her life. Phoebe goes off on her own, becomes an apprentice to the painter Walter Trale, and creates for herself a lively existence that Owen at first deplores, then admires, and finally resents. During this period, as part of her training as an artist, she executes a faithful copy of Walter's portrait of Elizabeth. She falls ill, and because of what Owen tells her doctor and psychiatrist, the illness is considered general and psychological, caused by a life of dissipation among artists—drugs, promiscuity, etc.—none of which is really true. Finally, the true nature of her illness is discovered,

she has to return to her parents' home in upstate New York, and she
undergoes a thyroidectomy on 15 August 1963. She despises Owen for
what he has done to her and takes revenge by humiliating him in various
ways, humiliations he in fact seeks, but ultimately she gives in to
her love for him. She dies in a hospital near her parents' home in the fall
of 1963.

(2) Lewis and Morris. Morris Romsen, at the age of 30, is already a
well-known art critic, and an essay of his on Walter Trale's painting
overwhelms Lewis Lewison. Lewis's sister Phoebe arranges a meeting
between the two men, which takes place at Trale's studio in September
1962. Lewis, 23 years old and drifting after college, is a masochist and
becomes involved in a public scandal when the police raid a sado-
masochist affair as he is being "crucified." Morris, rather than shunning
him, is very sympathetic, and they become lovers in a sado-masochistic
relationship. Because Irene Kramer, Morris's sister, is Walter Trale's
agent, both Morris and Lewis become closely connected with him, and a
sort of "substory" develops between Lewis and Walter. During the sixth
of their sado-masochistic evenings (23 May 1963) Morris encases Lewis
in concrete and then begins to taunt and insult and humiliate him.
Suddenly Morris has a heart attack, and Lewis, unable to move, watches
him die. The result is another public scandal. Walter's somewhat confused rejection of Lewis leaves him no one to turn to (his sister Phoebe is
critically ill in upstate New York at the time).

(3) Irene, Priscilla, and Walter. In the fall of 1961 Irene Kramer, the
older sister of Morris, opens an art gallery, and in the summer of 1962
she arranges two exhibitions of the work of Walter Trale. At first Trale
believes that Irene is in league with Morris and others to cheat him. At a
meeting with the two of them at his studio, during which he discovers
that he is wrong about Irene, Priscilla appears by coincidence for the first
time. Trale, who becomes famous as a result of the exhibitions, pursues
Irene relentlessly and she flees from him just as relentlessly. Priscilla, the
daughter of Allan and Maud Ludlam and just graduated from college
where she knew Phoebe, has come to the studio to bring Trale a copy of
her thesis, "The Female Figure in Recent American Art," which is mostly about him. She begins her pursuit of Trale, which is finally successful,
and they begin an affair that lasts for about a year. Jealous and fearing
that she will lose Walter, Priscilla indulges in intrigue to cut others out
of his life and ensure her own relationship with him. Thus she misleads
him and Irene about Morris and is largely responsible for a breach that
takes place between Walter and Lewis after Morris's death. Ultimately,

Walter (through Irene) discovers her deviousness, and their affair comes to an end. But she makes amends with Irene and goes to work for her.

(4) Allen and Owen. Morris in his will leaves everything to Priscilla (this because of his business partnership with her, but others are confused by or misinterpret the act). Allan Ludlam, Priscilla's father, drew up the will, and Irene, naturally suspicious, asks Owen Lewison, her lawyer, to look into the matter and determine if there was a breach of legal ethics. Owen discovers there was no such breach. Allan, who learns that Owen is investigating him, writes him, thanking Owen for having exonerated him. This strikes Owen as strange since Allan probably should be insulted by the investigation. Allan reacts the way he does because he had feared that Owen might be investigating his past, which includes a long history of insurance fraud. In the summer of 1963 the Ludlams purchase what everyone thinks is Trale's portrait of Elizabeth but which is, in fact, Phoebe's copy. Allan Ludlam, in an act of revenge against his wife, takes the portrait from his home to his apartment in the city. He calls Irene, from whom he bought it, reports it stolen, and asks if the gallery's insurance still covers it. When Owen hears of this, his suspicions *are* aroused ("No insurance broker would leave anything so valuable unprotected for two minutes, certainly not two weeks" [*Cigarettes*, 114]), and, in part because he loves a game and in part to escape the relationship between himself and his daughter Phoebe, he does begin an investigation and discovers the truth about Allan's past (Owen, it should be pointed out, launched his own successful business career with an insurance scam). Convinced that Allan would not destroy the painting, he makes use of Pauline Pruell (neé Dunlap, Maud's sister), who spends the night with Allan, finds the painting, and tells Owen. Owen confronts Allan with what he knows about his past and says he will not expose him if Allan gives him the portrait of Elizabeth. Allan capitulates. Owen first takes the portrait to Phoebe, then destroys it. The destruction is discovered by his son Lewis, who plans to use what he knows as revenge against Trale.

(5) Maud and Elizabeth. In July 1963, after her brief affair with Allan Ludlam (with which the novel began) Elizabeth on an impulse visits his wife Maud. Maud throws Allan out, Elizabeth moves in, and they become close friends, even to a certain extent lovers. They have a happy summer, Elizabeth helping Maud through hard times with her sister Pauline and her daughter Priscilla. But during the summer Elizabeth, while showing Maud how to ride, falls from a horse and injures her neck. Perhaps complications set in or, as a doctor says, perhaps an old injury is

responsible, but whatever the cause, Elizabeth suffers a severe stroke that leaves her paralyzed. She is brought back to Maud's house. Others come to visit. Maud, Walter, and Pauline are there—and a repentant Allan, just arrived, is peering through the screen door—when, in September 1963, Elizabeth dies.

(6) Other stories. I have concentrated on the action of 1962 to 1963 and in particular the summer of 1963, which begins with one death, ends with two, and during which most of the action and intrigue of the novel occurs. I have not told the stories as Mathews does but have extracted what seem to be the main stories. Mathews weaves them together in a manner that defies explication. But part of the pattern he weaves has to do with the past:

(a)    Louisa and Lewis. This account of the mother/son relationship provides the background for Lewis's masochism and his relationship with Morris.

(b)    Irene and Morris. This account of the brother/sister relationship parallels the account of Louisa and Lewis's relationship in providing the background for Morris's sadism.

(c)    Maud and Priscilla. The development of Priscilla's overambitious nature is presented ("Priscilla showed self-reliance from the time she could crawl. She saw the world as a nest of probable satisfactions. Obstacles . . . pointed toward bigger opportunities" [*Cigarettes*, 241]). This account of the mother/daughter relationship also provides links among the various stories, for example, the relationship between Priscilla and Lewis, described elsewhere, which occurs in the summer of 1954.[6]

(d)    Maud and Pauline. This section provides another view of the Oliver-Pauline courtship and marriage, primarily that of Maud. It examines the cause of the breach between the sisters and explains Pauline's behavior with Allan in the summer of 1963.

There are relationships that are alluded to but never explained or developed. For example, we are told that Oliver met Elizabeth through Louisa, and it may have been Louisa who introduced him to Pauline; we learn that Irene is an old friend of Maud, a very intriguing revelation since Irene and her brother Morris, who are the Jewish children of the owner of a chain of movie theaters, seem to have no family or social connections with the other characters before 1961. Minor events become significant (Allan, drunk, makes a pass at Elizabeth in 1936 and doesn't remember it), and someone who would seem at first to be a major character (Oliver) more or less drops out of the novel.

While Elizabeth would appear to be the main thread or "motif" (that is, Elizabeth not only as a person but as a work of art), Walter Trale would appear to be the most central character in the geometrical sense of a center around which everything revolves. Owen and Louisa's daughter Phoebe is his apprentice; Allan and Maud's daughter Priscilla is his lover; Irene is his agent; Morris and Lewis are, for a while, his friends; Oliver Pruell meets him in 1936; he is a good friend of Barrington Pruell, Oliver's father; Owen buys and destroys Phoebe's copy of his painting; at the end a relationship between him and Pauline seems to be developing. And of course it is he who paints the portrait of Elizabeth in 1936, the birth of his career as an artist signaling the beginning of the plot of the novel (or the other way around, of course, Elizabeth signaling the birth of his career).

There would seem to be no pattern or metaphorical structure to the time sequences in the novel. It does begin and end with the Maud-Allan-Elizabeth triangle; and, because Pauline is Maud's sister, one could make a case in which the first three sections balance the last three. That there are 15 sections means that the eighth, "Lewis and Walter," stands at the center, and coming just before and after it are, respectively, "Lewis and Morris" and "Louisa and Lewis." Since Lewis is the narrator and since it's plausible that Walter is the center of the novel, one could, I suppose, make something of their centrality in the structure. But how to account for the positioning of "Allan and Owen" or "Irene and Morris?" Not that the organization cannot be accounted for but that it can be accounted for in any number of ways. As I indicated earlier, my own paraphrasing of the main relationships was purely arbitrary. Of course, such a disruption of the chronological sequence makes it possible for Mathews to play games with the reader. For example, who is the woman in the "Allan and Owen" section referred to only as "High Heels?" Readers find out much later and then perhaps remember that they were told very early in the novel that the character has a nickname. (A similar game is played with the Lewis-Priscilla relationship.) But this minor game playing is secondary to the major game: Mathews provides one way to view the interactions of a group of people; it is, like any view of life, incomplete and the reader is left to invent his or her own causes and effects and coincidences and plausibilities.

## The Limits of Realism

Mathews often employs the analytical method of Realism, particularly premodernist Realism (though this, as we will see, needs qualification). Consider, for example, the following passage:

Their father had died that March, leaving his entire estate to his daugh-
ters. The orphaned sisters learned, in the weeks following his death, that
the conditions of their inheritance were known only to themselves and
their father's lawyers. No one else seemed aware that Mr. Dunlap had
amassed a great deal less than the many millions attributed to him, or
that, as a believer in primogeniture, he had bequeathed nine-tenths of his
fortune to his elder daughter. Since Maud was now married, the sisters
decided to keep these facts to themselves: Pauline might benefit from
appearing as a conspicuous heiress. (*Cigarettes*, 30)

The method is put to the service of "theme" or "idea," in this
instance, permutations of love in various relationships: mother/daughter,
mother/son, father/daughter, father/son, brother/sister, sister/sister, hus-
band/wife, man/man, woman/woman, man/woman. The only tradition-
ally close relationship omitted is, seemingly, brother/brother. The
analysis of love is detached and objective, balancing passion and compassion against the desire for power. At the center of the novel are the chapters devoted to Lewis and his masochism, which Mathews treats in an
understated, matter-of-fact way as a part of a genuine relationship, the
love between Lewis and Morris, a sadist.

The desire for power, for control, is what links the examination of love
in its various dimensions with money, another major motif or theme. In
her interview with Mathews, Lynne Tillman, referring to *Cigarettes*, says,
"So I wanted to talk about money," and Mathews replies: "Oh dear, really? I don't have much to say about money that isn't in the book. I guess
if I had to say something general about money, it would be that it's completely empty, it has no meaning in itself, no significance. It's simply in
reactions people have to it that it acquires an apparent role. It has no
inherent power." And later, when Tillman speaks of "the way in which
money figured in people's lives, people with money worrying about
money in some way," he replies, "It's an American hang up, I think"
(Tillman, 35).

On the one hand, the exchange indicates that Mathews is very much
a part of the people he writes about in this novel, people for whom earn-
ing money is not necessary for survival or even for a certain comfortable
level of existence but only as a counter in a game. This is not to say that
Mathews is more limited by his attitude toward money than any other
writer but only, as in every other writer's work, that Realism operates
within a limited sphere of reality. Thus when Tillman remarks, "This is
your most American novel, I thought," we shouldn't be surprised that

Mathews demurs slightly: "It's not the point of the novel at all. But I suppose socially that's true, in so far as it's a depiction of a social milieu" (Tillman, 35). For seen from another perspective, *The Sinking of the Odradek Stadium* is a much more "American" novel than *Cigarettes*.

Mathews is not unaware of the limitations that money puts not only on those who out of necessity must pursue it, but also on those who do not need to pursue it. When finishing the first draft of *Cigarettes* in 1984, he wrote in a kind of journal or notebook: "The next day you [Mathews himself] thought of reasons why R. might resent you—your money, his owing you money, the apparent ease of your life and your enjoyment of it, your having witnessed his despair last year."[5] By virtue of existing on a different material level, R. is estranged from Mathews, and paradoxically, the moral burden rests more heavily on Mathews the lender than on R. the borrower.

On the other hand, Mathews's attitude accounts, I think, for the fact that in all his novels money is both central and irrelevant. The main characters in *The Conversions* and *The Sinking of the Odradek Stadium* are driven (and perhaps destroyed) by the pursuit of money. In *Tlooth* the narrator's quest for revenge is often thwarted by her lack of money, a lack that drives her into the writing of an erotic screenplay. Yet in each of these cases the money is not necessary for survival; rather it is a means to an end, and that end is, in one way or another, power, one's power to control his or her own life. This is obvious as regards Zachary and the narrator of *The Conversions* and more subtle as regards the narrator of *Tlooth*, but even she seems content with her lot in life (music, dentistry) so long as she is not trying to effect revenge. Money is necessary to her desire for power over Roak. Only Twang seems to escape the lure of power: she is interested in the treasure more for Zachary's sake than for her own. Zachary, on the other hand, is convinced that money is necessary to the happiness of their relationship.

The obsession with money reaches its peak in *Odradek*, which chronicles confidence games played in the Middle Ages, the Renaissance, and contemporary times on two continents. And confidence games play an important role in *Cigarettes*, both literally—Allan makes use of them in his fraudulent dealings with insurance companies—and more subtly—emotional relationships are sometimes built on deception. But the reader is not likely to make the connection immediately or see right away that in fact confidence games were also important in *The Conversions* and possibly in *Tlooth* as well. This is not surprising. Mathews specializes in obvious clues and connections that turn out to be not so obvious and in opposites—seemingly unconnected people and events that turn out to be vitally connected.

## Love, Power, and Freedom

Love that includes the necessity for one partner to dominate the other is by no means confined to what most people think of as a perversion. The Lewis/Morris affair lies at the heart of the book in the sense that it branches out to all the other relationships. Lewis, writing about Irene, says, "[S]he knew that sadomasochism was hardly 'abnormal'" (*Cigarettes*, 220). Owen seeks to dominate and control Phoebe; Priscilla seeks to isolate Trale; Phoebe tortures her father; Allan uses Maud who in turn delights in taking revenge; Maud gives money to her sister and takes it away in unconscious or subconscious acts of generosity and meanness. And so on. The line between love and power is as fine as the linguistic distinction between *love* and *loathe*, a distinction made when Lewis, encased in concrete and watching his lover Morris die, hears him say, "[T]he truth is, and I'm singing it out, I lo— . . .," and "unhesitatingly grasped in its entirety: 'The truth is, I loathe you'" (*Cigarettes*, 152, 154). But of course, "loathe" really means "love" since Morris is saying it only to give both himself and Lewis pleasure.

The various relationships oscillate between the two poles represented by Elizabeth and Owen, the former spurning all desire for power and control, the latter incapable of any kind of relationship that is not based on one or the other. Owen, in his attempts to control others, actually effects their freedom; this may be even more true for Phoebe than for Allan. And Elizabeth, through her "saving" of Maud, brings the novel to a close on a note of unselfish love.

At certain points in the novel the characters rise above their various entrapments to experience glimpses of freedom. One of these "moments" is bound up with a lyrical celebration of nature:

> [Oliver] let the boat drift. He had no place to go. He did not
> think, except as part of the dreaming. Everything that had ever hap-
> pened was only seeming, a seeming of having been dreamed, not mat-
> tering, without matter. The boat rocked sleepily, turning this way and
> that, providing his feelings, his thoughts, their objects. For one moment
> quickly gone he tried to say what was happening to him (maybe Hegel,
> maybe Heine; they didn't matter either). He had nothing to grasp. He
> was surrounded entirely by the dream of his being. He was surrounded

by nothing. He did not need anything outside himself, outside this dream.

An hour passed. He gazed into the sky. The darkening grayness altered in the west. Above the silhouette of hills glowed low, scalloped reefs of emberish red. "Nothing outside us stays." Thought again subsided into the murk of woods and water, the clouds in their moment of fire and extinction looked to him like his own life being given shape, a hymn of pleasure and melancholy.

To the east the sky had assumed a darker and more soothing complexion: a slope of cool blue, or coal blue, the color that as a child he used to call policeman blue. He thought of the uncle the mention of whose name turned grown-ups silent, in disgrace, having squandered his money and his good marriage with other women. He was living in a suburb of Cleveland with a Mrs. Quilty. Blue, blue, policeman's blue. Oliver looked into the darkness and felt a shudder of power, realizing that his life belonged to him entirely, that there was no one else. He would never know such happiness again. (*Cigarettes*, 24)

Oliver's reverie juxtaposes a purely subjective vision of existence instilled by the beauty and serenity of nature against the intense objectivism of Mathews's descriptions of society. It is significant that Oliver, whose intuition, because he is only 22 at the time, makes him feel that anything is possible, drops out of the novel two years later, after he marries Pauline in 1938. But he returns metaphorically in that he is all the middle-aged characters of 25 years later, for one of whom another "moment" takes place on a subway train in 1963:

[Owen] turned away to consider someone nearer: a man with florid swollen features, short strawy hair above a shaved pink nape, a heavy belly that bulged through a half-untucked Hawaiian shirt over low-belted pants of shiny plaid synthetic gabardine—And so on, thought Owen, ad nauseam. Why did he mind? His own body felt warm and stupefied. He noticed that the light outside the train windows had become detached from his perception of it; and he saw that a similar hallucinatory change was occurring in his neighbor. He was separating into disjunct entities— still a looming, monstrous straphanger, while his eyes belonged to another body, another space: through them shined light from afar. A disjunct light existed behind the appearance the man turned to the world. That slob body had become an empty vessel with autonomous light inside it— a Halloween pumpkin. . . . He shyly glanced at others near him: veterans of one summer afternoon, each encased in his rind, each accumulating incongruities, pains, shames, even signs of happiness, to conceal that uncanny light—their masks, their lives. (*Cigarettes*, 60–61)

Here Oliver's dream of freedom becomes Owen's intuition that we
invent our reality, that we choose a mask and play a role. But middle-
aged, his own mask firmly in place, he is both frightened and disgusted
by his awareness of freedom.

His daughter Phoebe has her first "moment" not long after during
the sexual act, appropriately, since she is in her early twenties:

> The boy grunted knowingly. She let him be, surrendering to the soft
> tumult. She rose to meet and savor it, gliding through rings of splintery
> light, up, up. Where was she going? Higher, she found or mentally
> assembled webs of incandescence out of which the flakes came sprinkling.
> She guessed, she *knew* what they were: stars. The teetering stars had
> spilled into the gloom of her mind. She had no strength to resist that
> shower or the spidery filaments above it that sucked her in. She recog-
> nized where she had come: into the abstraction called love. She was being
> pelted with love and sucked into it—and this poor boy was still bumping
> against her. Sure he was. Love had been broken into bits among us, the
> way light was pieced out around the sky: here and there, the same thing.
> A showering, never fixed, except in a fixity of change, in the motion of its
> fragments. Each star moved in its ring, each man in his life each woman
> in her life, longing to touch and never able to, and still one life, one us.
> That's why I love cloudless nights, Phoebe thought. Truth was shining
> around her. She drifted into the welter of light. She laughed incredulous-
> ly, "It's us!" Her body shook with glee as he lost himself inside her.
> (*Cigarettes*, 84)

The complexity of Phoebe's vision goes far beyond the point I am trying
to make. Dominated as intimately as one can be dominated, she intuits
her freedom: in becoming one with the universe she finds "truth," her
own uniqueness. Being ill, she will attempt to hold her vision against the
assaults of both psychiatry and science.

## Games, Perspective, and Play

The illusion and reality of freedom, the mystery of the relationship
between the one and the many that winds through the novel in a subtle
theater motif, reaches its climax at the end when Lewis observes a man
in a train station. After two paragraphs of description of the man's
clothes and face, Lewis says: "The way he assumed his elegance implied
an imperiously debonair attitude to the world around him. He seemed to
be inventing his very presence here, imagining himself in some sublime

farce staged for the amusement of knowing friends, and for his own."
The observation would also be true of Allan, the solid insurance man
who has practiced fraud all his life; or of Owen, also respectable, who
began his career by cheating; or of Trale, worshipped as a wise man but
in fact no more than a child; or of Pauline, who in her act of revenge
"looked less like a dragon than like a lost lamb." But in this case we
learn that "the man I had seen in the station was a professional actor, not
particularly well known or successful except in his secondary career: he
appeared as a paid extra man at fashionable parties" (*Cigarettes*, 291).

Like Major Monarch in James's story "The Real Thing," the man in
the station contains several "realities": what he is (a man), what he does
(an actor), what he is and does (an actor turning his life and the lives of
others into a stage for his own enrichment). What makes him different
at parties where everyone is playing a role is that he doesn't possess what
"has no meaning in itself, no significance," money, the lack of which
places him in another world. But his "reality" depends on others as well.
To the people who hire him he is loneliness, failure, success, perversion,
necessity. To Lewis he is existence itself: an actor in a train station
becomes a metaphor for the soul's journey through life. Lewis is himself
"returning for the funerals," and the novel ends, like the Victorian novels before it whose structures were built on the rhythms of society and
custom—births and marriages and funerals—with death and a reverie
about the dead.

But it is *Lewis's* reverie, not that of an omniscient narrator as it most
likely would be in a nineteenth-century novel. And at the end we
remember that the novel began with Lewis as narrator: "I wanted to
understand. I planned someday to write a book about these people. I
wanted the whole story" (*Cigarettes*, 3). We are to assume, then, that
Lewis is the narrator, yet he functions as an omniscient narrator, recording events and thoughts he could not have experienced or in some cases
even heard about. In other words, Lewis "made it up." But so did all
those authors of Realistic novels. What the end of *Cigarettes* brings us
face to face with is the fact that every novel, every work of fiction, is told
from a first-person point of view. But because all of us desire to become
the ultimate voyeur, able to see everything, we attribute to the narrator
(the author) the omniscience of God. It is this conspiracy between author
and reader to create absolute truth that Mathews attacks at the end of
the novel. Simply falling into his own (Mathews's) voice would not do it;
often authors speak in the first person without losing their godlike
authority, so strong is the bond of omniscience. The return to Lewis

makes us realize what we have forgotten, that the "truth" about all these relationships had been Lewis's truth. Had Mathews begun with himself as speaker, lapsed into omniscience, and then returned to himself, readers would no more question the reality of what they have read than they do at the end of *Middlemarch* or *Pride and Prejudice*.

But not just any character will do as narrator in order for Mathews to make his point. Something similar to what happens in *Cigarettes* happens in *Moby-Dick*, which begins in Ishmael's voice, shifts to an omniscient narrator, and returns to Ishmael (who, somewhat like Lewis, is floating on a coffin). But Ishmael is a "reasonable man," ordinary, typical, and readers subconsciously equate him with Melville (who, as we all know, went to sea). Thus we patronize (the novel went through so many revisions that Melville forgot or ceased to care, but that's all right; it doesn't hurt the novel), or we say that Ishmael merges with, becomes, the ship, or we accept Ishmael as a "framing device" that in no way lessens the authority of the narrative voice. But Lewis is not ordinary or typical in the conventional meaning of those terms; he is a practicing masochist who in the course of the novel is crucified, goes in and out of rooms like a dog, is bound up like a hog and dragged around an apartment, and finally is encased in concrete and unable to aid his dying lover who curses him as he dies. It is doubtful that a reader, without hard evidence, will equate such a narrator with the author. In short, our rediscovery of Lewis as narrator, like our discovery about the narrator of *Tlooth*, forces us to go back and reread, reconsider, reevaluate what we have just finished.

The nature of that evaluation will depend in large measure on the reader. Certainly, some readers will be somewhat skeptical of an examination of love, passion, and power made by a masochist. Others will contend that Lewis is no more "perverted" than anyone else. And still others will contend that his obvious intellectual and aesthetic abilities override his predilections and prejudices. In other words, Lewis will have whatever power the reader gives him. Mathews says: "[O]f writer and reader, the reader is the only creator. This is how reading can be defined: an act of creation for which the writer provides the means."[6] The means in this instance being several complicated entanglements and a somewhat unusual narrator.

Mathews, then, works within the tradition of modernism in his skeptical treatment of Realism. Though his starting point in *Cigarettes* would seem to be that "representation" or "realism" he considers a "dubious" point of departure, he himself rejects the notion that the novel is finally Realism (Ash, 32). The problem raised by the novel would seem to be the old one, closure. How does one end a work that deals with "relation-ships." Mathews approaches the problem in part as a modernist: he uses a framing device (the narrator), patterns of imagery (birds and paintings, for example), alteration of the time sequence (begins at the end, jumps back halfway, then all the way, then forward past the "end" to the pre-sent). Taken together, these devices lessen the slice of life effect and give the work a unity rooted not in time but in idea—a philosophical novel. He breaks down the tyranny of time in an ironic fashion, by calling our attention to it.

The irony runs even deeper. In altering the time sequence Mathews moves, in the terms of E. M. Forster, from storytelling to plot. Whereas in the first two novels he used a simple conventional story line to string together a series of tales, in *Cigarettes* he breaks a simple story line into a series of juxtaposed fragments that call attention to cause-and-effect relationships, some of the most conventional type, (e.g., the psychologi-cal effect on Lewis of the conduct of his parents). And plot, in its attempt to impose an order on reality, introduces the dimension of play. *Play* is, or has become, a very broad term, encompassing practically everything from volleyball to Christianity. In *Cigarettes*, although Mathews probably makes use of several of its manifestations, two seem important: the theater motif, and play as it applies to game.

To take the second first, we have seen Mathews make use of games in specific ways in the earlier novels. And in each of those novels we have seen how game is infused into the very structure of the novel and actual-ly serves to move the reader outside the text to his or her own act of cre-ation. In *Cigarettes*, as Mathews points out (Ash, 31), most specific game playing drops out, but the plot constitutes a game, the boundaries and rules of which govern the reader's act of creation. Minor mysteries—why does Oliver drop out? Why are only the first three letters of Elizabeth's last name given?—and major mysteries—Why does Allan practice fraud? Why does Lewis want to write *this* novel?—are finally contained in the game set up by Mathews: What is the "reality" of this group of people who do these things during this period of time?

*Play* in this novel, however, also encompasses the old stage, or dra-matic, metaphor so common in drama, fiction, and poetry. The master-ful ending of *Cigarettes* is most relevant here: "I sometimes think that only the residual strength of the dead beings inside me gives me power to survive at all. By that I mean both the accumulated weight of the generations succeeding one another and, as well, from the first of times, when names held their objects fast and light shone among us in miracles

of discovery, the immortal presence of that original and heroic actor who
saw that the world had been given him to play in without remorse or
fear" (*Cigarettes*, 292).

This is a fine summary not only of the ideas and attitudes of this book
but of Mathews's fiction up to the time of its writing. It alludes to the
problem of language, of the relationship between words and reality, that
underlies his ideas and suggests that at least one task of the writer is to
make us "discover" reality (or as Mathews would probably put it, to provide the material for discovery). The discovery of reality, moreover, is a
"miracle," yet at the same time discovery grows out of time: the past, all
"the generations succeeding one another," form a bridge back to what
exists in each of us, "that original and heroic actor who saw that the
world had been given him to play in without remorse or fear."

Yeats once said that we do not begin to live until we conceive of life as
a tragedy. One of the many things he meant by this is that we are capable of conceiving of a perfection we can never achieve in this world. Thus
"this world" becomes an arena in which all of us, playing by the rules—
both consciously and unconsciously—make our discoveries. And referring to his own games, perhaps Mathews speaks for all his "creators," his
readers: "[A]ll these activities were means to express my passionately
held idea of the truth" (Interview).

## An American Writer

This last statement is characteristic of Mathews. Whereas most writers would have said, "to express the truth," Mathews, simultaneously the
Fideist and the Defective Baptist, steps back as he plunges in by adding,
"my passionately held idea," "passionately" emphasizing emotional
involvement, "idea" a devotion to the dictates of reason. Who, after all,
*knows* the truth? It is such balance, I think, that causes Ash to remark,
"When I first read your work I felt I had discovered a path which had
not been followed, at least not in the English novel, and not by the
mainstream anywhere" (Ash, 22). For though Ash goes on to say, "It was
the path of wit and artifice, of fantastic inventions and intellectual play,"
he must mean something more because all these have been, at one time
or another, at least part of the mainstream of the English novel. And
when he says, "Many of [m]y favorite European and Latin-American
writers were somehow present in your work—Kafka, Walser, Borges,
Nabokov, Calvino and so on," he identifies one side of Mathews's fiction
and adds, "you were never merely derivative" (Ash, 22).

English, European, Latin American—Mathews seems to echo certain twentieth-century concerns of each culture but, despite a lifetime in France, seems outside all these cultures. Mathews says about the effects of living in France, "You're forced to be conscious of your language and your writing and your attitude toward writing" (Ashbery, 45). And though he pays homage to Mallarmé and Roussel, he asserts his independence from them in this interview. In fact, a key to Mathews's originality is so obvious it is easy to overlook: he is an American writer.[7]

In her interview with him, Tillman asked Mathews, "How did you see that move [to France in 1952] then and how do you see it now?" Mathews's reply is worth quoting at length:

> When I first left America I was very happy to leave the country and what I have to immediately add to that is that I didn't know the country and I didn't even know New York City, what I knew was the life of the well-to-do Upper East Side and that life seemed very discouraging to me in terms of what I wanted to do. . . . [W]hen I went down to what later became my stamping grounds, Greenwich Village, among painters, I felt so far out of my element, I felt even worse there than I did among the Upper East Side crowd . . . so then I went to Europe. It was like a kind of going into exile . . . although what it really felt like was going back to a place which was very familiar and which had been sort of mysteriously familiar. I didn't come back to the United States at all for six years and then I came back a little bit, I didn't like it and then I came back a little bit more and liked it a little bit more, and of course by then I'd met John Ashbery and through him many other friends here and I was discovering a whole other aspect of New York City and the country. I don't know America very well, I haven't traveled it nearly as much as I'd like to, but that original aversion to it vanished. And in any case, even if my departure might have been a kind of expatriation at the beginning, it never amounted to a separation from my identity as an American. I've never been anything else, I've never thought of myself as being anything else. . . . I very quickly learned that you never leave home. And I think the great advantage of having gone to Europe and having lived there is that it allowed me to become more aware of my American-ness than I would have if I had stayed here. (Tillman, 36)

What Mathews says reveals the abiding belief that there is such a thing as "America" and such a being as "an American." This belief is held in the face of an overwhelming reality, for when Mathews says, "I don't know America very well," and immediately adds, "I haven't traveled it nearly as much as I'd like to," he speaks of America outside New

York City as one would speak of a foreign country and of the need to travel in it to know it, which can mean knowing it only in a limited sense, as one "knows" a foreign country. And when he says of his "American-ness," "I've never been anything else, I've never thought of myself as anything else," he means something quite different from what Walker Percy or Joan Didion would mean if either said the same thing. Something similar is true of any nation, but it is more true of the United States, which has no tradition or belief to hold together its fluctuating and changing cultures. It's not surprising that when Mathews in his writing ventures outside New York for an American setting, he goes to Miami. This lack of a nation is not, of course, the lack of a place, a culture, a home. But it is difficult to come to grips with the fact that nothing binds "America" together but politics. Americans may not know or think this, but they intuit it, as when Mathews, discussing his reasons for leaving the United States, says: "In 1952 I ran away from America. Which was not America: it was the milieu in which I'd been raised, and I thought that's what America was, that is to say, an upper-middle-class Eastern WASP environment, which I read as being extremely hostile to the poetic and artistic enthusiasms that I felt were most important at that time" (Ashbery, 46).

In fact, though that "environment" wasn't America in the sense that any segment of France, in some way or another, is France, it was and still is a very real and important part of America. Significantly, Ashbery immediately associates that environment with politics ("That was a sort of low point in America"), and Mathews agrees, citing "McCarthyism," which Ashbery equates with the "New Right." This produces from Mathews an attack on American "values" (i.e., values of the McCarthy era and of the New Right). But still Mathews has "never felt that I was anything but an American," and he hopes that, as an "American-living-abroad," he can still "contribute to what's happening [in the U.S.] as much as anyone else" (Ashbery, 46).

One cannot generalize about the relationship between the artist and his "environment." Faulkner probably wouldn't have written his great novels if he hadn't lived most of his life in the place of his birth, and Joyce probably wouldn't have written his if he had not left that place. But one can trace Mathews's "American-ness" through his novels. The first three reflect the wit and artifice of the detached personality, neither affirming nor denying place (or by extension time). They issue from a vision that exhibits a great knowledge of history but no sense of history (which does not mean that Mathews has no sense of history). The games, unlike those played by European writers, seem grounded in something that is almost tragic. It is, in short, the vision of the alienated European but, unlike Conrad or Joyce, alienation by virtue of politics, not birth.

In *Cigarettes*, set entirely in the twentieth century in New York with no overt use of mythology or history, there emerges a genuine sense of the past, a sense that grows out of place, geography. Mathews writes of America not as a nation but as *home*. Many of the games of the earlier novels—linguistic, confidence, religious, etc.—emerge once again but in a new context. So when Tillman observes, "This is your most American novel," and Mathews replies, "It's not the point of the novel at all," paradoxically he makes Tillman's point for her.

This is not to say that *Cigarettes* is better than the previous novels; only time will decide that. But *Cigarettes* is the culmination, at this time, of Mathews's fiction, of his American-ness, a quality that has always governed his writing, a quality very much a part of the idea of truth that he has always "passionately held."

# Chapter Seven
# Realism, Games, and Ritual

## The Return of Realism?

Tom Wolfe stirred up much controversy when he published "a literary manifesto for the new social novel."[1] Actually calling for a return to the old social novel of Dickens, Zola, George Eliot, Balzac, etc., he excoriated the "Puppet-Masters . . . in love with the theory that the novel was, first and foremost, a literary game, words on a page being manipulated by an author" (Wolfe, 49). As many of the writers and critics who responded to the article pointed out,[2] Wolfe greatly oversimplified in order to make his point, and in his response to the letter writers he attempted to defend such a writer as Faulkner as a "realist," thus compounding one oversimplification with another.

Such controversies are harmless enough. Perhaps they even stir up interest in "literature." But generally they have very little to do with literature because they assume that writers are controlled by their environment. Moreover, the controversialists create the environment to which they believe the writers respond. Thus Wolfe: "After the Second World War, in the late 1940s, American intellectuals began to revive a dream that had glowed briefly in the 1920s. They set out to create a native intelligentsia on the French or English model, an intellectual aristocracy—socially unaffiliated, beyond class distinctions—active in politics and the arts. In the arts, their audience would be the inevitably small minority of truly cultivated people as opposed to the mob, who wished only to be entertained or to be sure they were 'cultured.' By now, if one need edit, the mob was better known as the middle class" (Wolfe, 47). Note that Wolfe says not some or many or most, but simply "American intellectuals." And later he does the same when he asserts, "[T]he intelligentsia have always had contempt for the realistic novel." Though some intellectuals can become an intelligentsia that is influential, they can work their will only on mediocre writers; genius in the long run shapes the intelligentsia.

Of course, by "realism" Wolfe mean representation. Mathews, very aware of the attitude toward fiction exhibited by Wolfe, observes: "Americans are usually very upset when you start talking about literature as words being maneuvered in a certain way. . . . [T]hey feel it's either a game, or it's frivolous, or it may be interesting, but it isn't the real thing" (McPheron, 199). Obviously, any book *is* "words on a page manipulated by an author." Some authors manipulate words in order to imitate reality, others to transform reality, and still others to obscure or distort reality. Surely what is crucial is how successful the author is at manipulating words. Perhaps young writers of the 1960s didn't reject Sinclair Lewis because he was a realist (as Wolfe asserts) but because they thought that he was a bad realist. And perhaps they were drawn to Borges because many of his "fantasies" are realistic in the most profound sense.

Wolfe's essay is useful because it raises in an intelligent way the question of "realism" in literature, a question Mathews has addressed several times, and because it raises the question of realism as regards *American* literature, Wolfe believing that an American writer has a duty to *represent* American life by grounding his art in accurate reporting (Wolfe, 52–53). Certainly none of Mathews's novels, whether they treat American life or not, is grounded in reporting (in the journalistic sense of the word). In fact, just the opposite would seem to be true. At first glance, Mathews appears to be one of the writers that Wolfe attacks when he writes: "Other Neo-Fabulists wrote modern fables, à la Kafka, in which the action, if any, took place at no specific location. You couldn't even tell what hemisphere it was. It was some nameless, elemental terrain—the desert, the woods, the open sea, the snowy wastes. The characters had no backgrounds. They came from nowhere. They didn't use realistic speech. Nothing they said, did, or possessed indicated any class or ethnic origin. Above all, the Neo-Fabulists avoided all big, obvious sentiments and emotions, which the realistic novel, with its dreadful Little Nell scenes, specialized in" (Wolfe, 49–50). While Mathews generally uses real (actual) places in his novels, these locations are often of no great importance beyond certain superficial qualities (Venice, Sfax). Or he uses a real place in order to create another, imaginary, place. Thus Miami in *The Sinking of the Odradek Stadium* becomes a wonderful fantasy of real place names mixed with totally incongruous places and events. And in *Tlooth* we have a carefully mapped journey through actual geographical locations, yet that journey begins in a Soviet prison camp named Jacksongrad.

In his most recent novel Mathews does use what Wolfe would identify as "realism," a faithful representation of a certain segment of society.
But while Mathews acknowledges the realism in *Cigarettes*, he is, as we
have seen, somewhat hesitant to identify it as a realistic novel, the reason
being not only the alteration of the time sequence (the game he invents)
but also a deep-seated suspicion of the term *Realism* because of all the
social and political connotations the word carries. Since a novel is a
manipulation of words on the page, the relation of those words to "real
life" can never be simply a matter of representation, let alone reporting.

Yet another reason for his suspicion of Realism lies in Mathews's belief
that it is the reader, not the writer, who produces whatever "realism" a
work possesses. One of the problems with Realism is that it has done
much to develop the lazy reader. As long ago as the last decade of the
nineteenth century, W. W. Canning, discussing the modern reader's
inability to comprehend Milton's prose, observed: "To be universally
intelligible is not the highest merit. A great mind cannot, without inju-
rious constraint, shrink itself to the grasp of common, passive readers."[3]
Realism, for all its achievements, has done much to increase this passivity. Probably most readers in any age are incapable of intense involvement in what they are reading, just as most writers are probably
incapable of providing material for such involvement. But Realism, especially the kind Wolfe champions, encourages passivity by postulating a
writer who assembles details gathered from accurate observation to produce a world for the reader. At most the reader is involved only to the
extent of matching the assembled world with the "real" one—that is,
the world as the reader knows it. When Wolfe states, "The effect on the
emotions of everyday realism such as Richardson's was something that
had never been conceived of before," one can only ask, "Why?" Why
didn't the Greeks, who judged art on the basis of its fidelity to nature,
not "conceive of it" in literature—at least in the theater and the epic?
Even their comedy, which dealt with contemporary social and political
issues, never abandoned poetic form. No writer sought to capture the
everyday reality of his society more fervently than Dante, yet in the
*Commedia*, though he chose the vernacular, he also chose terza rima. To
say that prose was not an accepted literary form is to beg the question.

All other ages have considered "reality" to be bound up with form,
with convention. And one of the main reasons for the formation of the
Oulipo (*Ouvroir de Littérature Potentielle*), which Mathews became a member of in 1972, was to explore the possibility ("potential") for literature
grounded in conventions, which are what "constraints" come to be called

after they are accepted and become a part of the mainstream. As Mathews himself notes, most of his tendencies in fiction were established before his election (he had already written *The Conversions* and *Tlooth*), but certainly the organization did much to deepen his enthusiasm for literature as *play*.

## The Short Fiction

That enthusiasm in its purest form is evident in his short fiction, which would seem to be the sort of writing that Wolfe attacks. In "The Network,"[4] for example, he plays with artificial transitional devices, manipulating three of them (however, anyway, moreover) in the following manner: "hahmhahmhahmhahmhahmhahmhahmha." This suggests a constraint: a pattern similar to the poetic devices of stanza, rhyme, and refrain. But upon closer examination one discovers that, surprisingly, the repetition contains no truly completed pattern. And since none of the three words is used consistently to end a sentence or a paragraph, one would guess that Mathews is using the arrangement as a counterpoint to the usual divisions in prose.

If the arrangement is a constraint used by Mathews to force himself into novel modes of expression,[5] what it produces is an obscure account of bodily functions. Perhaps what is being described is drunkenness: "In a daze, however, as good as death or a bad cold, crossed the avenue from that café. Had forgotten, moreover, to piss. Resorted to a hotel lobby, however . . . a flight of metal steps led down into powdery dusk, in an atmosphere of steamship depths, through which gazed anyway from a warm railing. . . . The sensation of upheaval was not missing" (*Stories*, 59–60). If so then it may be followed by a search for a way to describe the pain, "for a defining concept, such as 'derrick hook in back.' . . . There was the jolt, the jolting effect anyway, that also contained the pain" (*Stories*, 60). Or perhaps "steamship depths" is intended to be metaphorical in some other way: perhaps we are given a descent into the body itself, ending with "transferral," which "took place in three stages, with wall flake, pipe bundles, and lone bulbs passing in a detached flatness, perhaps from the loss of depth perception or of one eye: first, laterally to a position among swaying cables; second, upwards, to be glued to a joist; third, far down, finally moored anyway to the cloth hide of a pipe, with hot hushed rushing" (*Stories*, 61). "[D]reaming followed . . . peering from the sheet cavern; hunting cool pillow areas," but it is the kind of dreaming that occurs "in dozy reading, e.g.: measles nap—green gloom. . . . The pipe was, moreover, *hot*—will it scorch? However can't care but not in its interest." Certainly the penultimate paragraph could well be a description of passing out: "The spine pain anyway is fixed throughout the length of the body forever, it has been decided. What about sleep, however?" And the final paragraph might well carry on that sensation: " . . . a summer swim, climbing onto a bank to dry, stickily moreover . . . floating . . . in a medium like water, and like air . . . " (*Stories*, 61–62). But as usual one cannot be sure. At times "The Network" sounds more like a description of a medical procedure: "[T]he swathing had commenced. Already there was, however, no more notion of time spans. It was done with a supple tape, not describable as wet (the point is doubtful anyway because of the novocaine drench)" (*Stories*, 60).

"The Ledge" has even less narrative movement, real or imagined, than "The Network." In one long paragraph it describes the action of fog and cloud during the course of a single day. Beginning at dawn, the description first follows the fog vertically and horizontally; then, when the "truer clouds" appear, the description becomes geographical—north, south, east, west. The description opens with dawn and closes with "the night sky." All in all, the visual effects of the prose are superb.

Yet the piece is titled "The Ledge," which calls attention not to what is described but to the vantage point and, inevitably, to the viewer. Just as the title "The Network" subtly alludes to the poemlike pattern of the narrative (the constraint), so "The Ledge" points to technique, in this instance point of view, which may well act as a kind of constraint. For while the viewer remains stationary, the essence of the description is movement: "[The fog] rose steadily, in silver layers, like jellyfish gliding toward the surface of the ocean . . . a bunched white river of cloud . . . flowed south . . . loglike clouds surged as the day warmed. . . . [The clouds] did not cling in the forests but pushed over them, and even the hills did not alter the direction, only the inclination, of their advance" (*Stories*, 78–80). Even when the clouds do come to a standstill, their lack of movement is more apparent than real. Thus the clouds in the west seem to be motionless yet when the viewer looks away for a moment and then looks back, "although still flat and immobile, they were in new parts of that section of the sky." The clouds "rolled, flattening as they sank, slowly around from north to west. . . . [O]ne vast layer . . . slides over the hilltops . . . like smoke from dry ice." Yet throughout the day the viewers "on the edge of the plateau, remained indefatigably vigilant" (*Stories*, 80–81).

This description of the vantage point, which occurs three-fourths of the way through the paragraph, also contains the first direct mention of a person, a viewer ("we"). Indeed, the reader is over halfway through the piece before there is any suggestion of a viewer, and even then it is submerged in a use of the passive voice that verges on ungrammatical construction: "Stared at, [the clouds] were never seen to alter their position or shape. . . . Yet after a glance to the north . . . the western clouds had become unrecognizable." And shortly thereafter, "It was to those northern apparitions . . . that attention was directed" (*Stories*, 80). Only after the scene has become a "spectacle . . . at once satisfyingly dramatic and satisfyingly remote" are we reminded that what we are seeing is being described by someone and that whatever "reality" it has depends on someone's perspective. And it is only when that perspective is firmly established that the speaker begins to sound less like a dramatist and more like a painter: "[The clouds] changed in color from cold-gray-tinged white through strawy yellow, in which the gray took on a darker tone, faint gold, rust, and red to black, black at first streaked with sunset hues, then thick black" (*Stories*, 80–81). As in *Cigarettes* Mathews reminds us that there is no such thing as an omniscient point of view, that even the most basic kind of description is subjective.

In the title of the collection he refers to these and the other works as "stories," but in them narrative and conflict are subordinate to the relationship between narrative voice and idea, a relationship that usually depends upon play for its effect. Though all the stories, with the exception of "Tradition and the Individual Talent" and possibly "The Novel as History," are told in the first person, the narrator is absorbed in a context that alters considerably the conventions of first-person point of view established through the development of the tradition of Realism.

For example, "The Dialect of the Tribe" is cast in the form of a letter in which the narrator accepts an invitation to "contribute to the Festschrift in your honor." The person to whom he is writing is apparently a novelist whose work the narrator has translated. After accepting the invitation, the narrator turns to a "coincidence—only minds poorer than ours would call it accident" and relates how he discovered a text in "Pagolak, the speech of a small hill tribe in northern New Guinea" (*Stories*, 40, 41). The rest of the letter is taken up with the narrator's account of *Kalo Gap Pagolak*, "an oral declaration by the *abanika* or 'chief word-chief' of the tribe" (*Stories*, 43): "The text . . . was an account of a method used by the Pagolak-speaking tribe to translate their tongue into the dialects of their neighbors. What was remarkable about this method was that while it produced translations that foreign listeners could understand and accept, it also concealed from them the original meaning of every statement made" (*Stories*, 41–42).

The narrator found the language itself "accessible enough" and expected to be able to produce quickly a translation of the *Kalo Gap Pagolak*, but he discovered that "inherent in the very utterance of Pagolak was something that kept the roughest translation beyond my grasp" (*Stories*, 42). Finally, he decided that he could not translate the text: "Was it after all so surprising for a language to resist ordinary procedures of translation when it was itself capable of extraordinary ones? What could be more extraordinary than a method that would allow words to be 'understood' by outsiders without having their substance given away?" (*Stories*, 43–44). Moreover, it wasn't only the *abanika* who could control the method "but every last member of his tribe. . . . It was an integral part of the language itself." Thus the narrator, in learning Pagolak, discovers that, like the natives, he can understand what the *abanika* said but cannot translate it into any other language. "The *abanika*'s declaration . . . was not an account of the process, it was the process itself. And how can you translate a process?" The "process" is embodied in "*kalo gap*, the 'magic changing,' the redirecting of language towards foreign ears in a way that both provides clarity and suppresses translation's customary *raison d'être*—the communication of substantive content." An explanation and analysis of this "process" being impossible, the narrator can only "describe, suggest, record" its "impressions and effects" (*Stories*, 44–45), which he proceeds to do, closing with a passage in Pagolak.

Some of the characteristics of the language suggest that Mathews is using it as metaphor. Pagolak both reveals and conceals, and this is a function of the language itself, not a manipulation of the language by an "expert." The language makes impossible "the communication of substantive content" (*Stories*, 45). Thus one can understand what someone says only if one speaks the language of that person. In all this there is nothing particularly new or unusual. Everyone knows that any translation can be no more than an approximation, if that. But when the narrator goes on to say "that translation may, precisely, exorcise the illusion that substantive content exists at all" (*Stories*, 45), he indicates a much more radical view, that language *is* content and what we call "reality" can only be our interpretation not of nature but of words. And though the narrator refers to the Pagolak language as "extraordinary," he implies later that it is extraordinary only in that it is a primitive language: "[B]ut what led a remote New Guinean tribe to such a discovery? Why should it care?" (*Stories*, 45). The answer would seem to be that "such a discovery" lies in the origin of language itself. Thus McPheron, quoting taped interviews, states, "[Mathews] understands . . . language as an instrument serving not 'to represent [or] show meaning but actually determine it'" (McPheron, 198).

That the narrator does not believe that there is any such thing as "substantive content" takes us away from the language game and back to the story. The narrator is after all a translator who, in writing a letter to a fiction writer or poet, says that "while [translation] differs enormously in substance from true writing (like your own), the difference is only one of degree. One might then say that insofar as true writing *is* a kind of translation, the text from which it works is an infinitely arduous one: nothing less than the universe itself" (*Stories*, 40). The artist's "text" ("substance") is "the universe"; the translator's "text" ("substance") is what the artist has written. If "substantive content" is an "illusion," then both nature and works of art are "texts" that contain no substance. The only reality that language "represents" is the reality we ascribe to it.

A similar idea seems to be at work in "Remarks of the Scholar Graduate," another first person narration, but this time cast in the form of a lecture. The speaker explains what he considers his great contribution to the field of language studies: his discovery that the alphabet of the ancient Bactrians, and ultimately our own "international alphabet," developed from and through purely spatial characteristics, "the horizontal line, or dash," which "was a non-phonetic symbol of the ancient Bactrian divinity, derived from its incarnation as a snake (Stories, 64)." The number of such "lines" varied and many of them were not strictly horizontal. So what seem to the reader to be nothing more than scratches come, in the theory of the speaker, "to stand . . . for the *name* of the god as well as for the god himself." Such an assertion enables him to interpret a vertical group (column) of seven dashes not simply as repetition; dismissing what he considers the "dead-end street" of "giving importance to physical variations of the sign," he insists that "the dashes are *not* identical": "The dash at the bottom is, uniquely, the dash at the bottom. The one above it is not at the bottom, and by that virtue is unlike the first. The one above that is similarly distinct from the two below it. So it goes through the topmost one." This is his one "original idea," and "the rest of my hypothesis flowed naturally from it" (*Stories*, 66–68).

The narrator says that he next concluded that the Bactrians "posited a phonetic significance to this differentiation" (*Stories*, 68), assigning consonant sounds to the dashes and vowel sounds to the spaces between the dashes and reading from bottom to top. What resulted was a language of one—and only one—written word, "pafosutishelak," the name of the Bactrian divinity, "which was affixed to all things, so that all things bore the name of god" (*Stories*, 70–71).

Soon there occurred a shift from one to several columns, and from this development the narrator concluded that "as the position of the dashes in a column determined their function, so the positions of the columns in a line determines theirs" (*Stories*, 72). It is impossible to know "whether the words were all the same while their denotation silently varied; or whether the words themselves changed with their denotations" (*Stories*, 72). But all statements "were obliged to begin with the words 'God copulates with the soul of (the) mother,' this was in fact the cardinal sense of all declarations. . . . [W]e may say that where in the first period Bactrian writing consisted of one divine name that was identified with all things, in the second period it consisted of a statement of one divine act that was identified with all acts" (*Stories*, 74).

After this development the system crumbled: "Groups were divided into fractions that represented an increasingly various number of phonetic objects, including vowels, diphthongs, and syllables. . . . These fractions lost more and more of their relation to the original sounds of the groups, and of course to the sacred meanings of the original words, or word" (*Stories*, 75–76). Vertical or diagonal marks began to appear, and finally the "last reminder of its origins [the seven levels of the dashes] disappeared from the alphabet (for such it now was)" (*Stories*, 76).

The narrator asserts that "ten Bactrian characters survive in the modern international alphabet of our own time; . . . they occupy the first six positions in it, as well as—and this is the most telling of all—the first and the last" (*Stories*, 77). Thus the language we speak quite possibly had its origin in what the reader is likely to see as meaningless scratches given spurious significance by an ambitious scholar.

In one sense "The Dialect of the Tribe" and "Remarks of the Scholar Graduate" are in the mainstream of current linguistic theory and debate. And the fact that Mathews casts them in the form of "stories" merely emphasizes that what they assert is finally no more absolute than any other assertion, a commonplace of much contemporary criticism. For example, it is possible to read "The Dialect of the Tribe" as a study in the degeneration of culture. The narrator quotes Herodotus as saying, "The

few remaining Old Bactrians say that until the time of the calamity they
wrote with a single letter [the name of their god]. Some attribute their
demise to the abandonment of the original practice" (*Stories*, 67). As the
language developed, it lost its relation "to the sacred meanings of the
original words, or word," and the last trace of this relationship ended
"just before the destruction of the Bactrian state and the dispersion of its
people" (*Stories*, 76). Or one could make the opposite argument, that the
development of language was part of, perhaps the cause of, an upward
evolution. The shift from a writing that "consisted of one divine name"
to one that "consisted of a statement of one divine act" is paralleled by a
similar shift in "religious belief from a magical to a moral god" and "in
economy from agriculture to trade" (*Stories*, 74). How we interpret either
of these "stories" depends on how we interpret the character of the narrator.

Manipulation of point of view is carried to an extreme in what is
probably Mathews's best-known piece of short fiction, "Country
Cooking from Central France: Roast Boned Rolled Stuffed Shoulder of
Lamb (*Farce Double*)." Where "The Dialect of Tribe" is a letter accepting
an invitation to contribute to a festschrift, and "Notes of the Scholar
Graduate" is a lecture, "Country Cooking" takes the form of a recipe. In
typical fashion, Mathews maintains the appearance of the recipe
throughout by alluding (as in *The Conversions*) to things that do not
appear in the text ("see *Appendix*," "see *stock*," "explained on p. 888," "an
object the size of this cookbook"). As regards the recipe itself, the reader
will have to determine to what extent Mathews's punning on *"farce double"* (described later) should be applied to it. But within the limits (constraint?) of a recipe, Mathews develops a *tour de force* that contains several
"stories."

First and most obviously, "Country Cooking" is a frame story in
which the recipe is used to encase an old folktale (actually a song).
During the five-hour wait while the lamb is roasting, "the genial cooks
of La Tour Lambert may fall to drinking, dancing and singing. . . . One
song always sung . . . tells the story of a blacksmith's son who sets out to
find his long-lost mother" (*Stories*, 24). The narrator then tells this story
of the young man's search, which involves three treacherous women,
each of whom "does for him what mother never did for her son," "burly
villains," a witch, a number of killings, etc. Finally, returning home, he
meets a shepherdess who is in love with him, and she "does for him what
mother never did for her son." Later, as they are lying side by side and
staring up at the stars, she tells him that "his mother lives beyond the

stars, and the stars themselves are chinks in the night through which the
fateful light of the dead and the unborn is revealed to the world." She
then tells him that "from this night on I alone am your mother—even if
now, and tomorrow, and all the days of my life, I do for you what mother never did for her son" (*Stories*, 29–30).

That such a story should be included in a recipe is, of course, absurd.
And yet it seems to emerge naturally from the context of the recipe
because, almost from the beginning, the narrator has been giving us not
only the recipe but also the history and culture of La Tour Lambert, the
town in which the dish originated. Before we hear about the song, we
have learned, among other things, that shepherds in Auvergne pick
juniper berries "in late summer when they drive their flocks from the
mountain pastures" (*Stories*, 11), how the natives fish, what the women
look like as they enter and leave the cave where cream is stored, how the
boys who participate in the cooking are honored ("every Sunday
throughout the following year, they will be allowed to wear their unmis-
takable lily-white smocks" [*Stories*, 21]), how "senior cooks" in the town
stand on "high stepladders" as they "shift the animal" (*Stories*, 23). Thus
the story of the young man's search is part not only of a recipe but of
another story, the story of La Tour Lambert, which was once a charming
village but has now, we are told at the end, "undergone considerable
change": sheep are no longer driven by shepherds but are shipped by
truck, lakes have been fished out, most of the young people have left, a
cement quarry employs mostly foreigners and "shroud[s] the landscape
in white dust." But the future of *farce double* is assured because "the fes-
tal cave has been put on a commercial footing, and it now produces the
dish for restaurants in the area all year round (in the off season, on week-
ends only)" (*Stories*, 37–38).

The person who tells us all this is the author of a cookbook, and he
(or she) begins in a manner typical of many such publications: "Here is
an old French regional dish for you to try . . . the specialty of La Tour
Lambert, a mountain village in Auvergne, that rugged heart of the
Massif Central. I have often visited La Tour Lambert. . . . I have observed
the dish being made and discussed it with local cooks" (*Stories*, 9–10).
Soon, however, the writer tells us that "an incurable stickler" can find
the molds to shape the quenelles in the form of birds "in any of the better head shops" (*Stories*, 16). And when the writer warns the reader
against drinking during the five-hour roasting period, anyone familiar
with Mathews's work will remember the cooking scene in *The Sinking of
the Odradek Stadium* and begin to suspect that the author is not a typical

cookbook writer. This suspicion is strengthened when the writer describes how a native of La Tour Lambert, upon being told that plastic is sometimes used to envelop the quenelles, fell into a marinating trough, and "[d]ripping oil, encrusted with fragrant herbs, he emerged briskly and burst into tears" (*Stories*, 17).

This narrative voice provides the ambiguity so typical of Mathews's work. The narrator's immediate explanation of the relevance of the old folk song seems tenuous to the point of absurdity: "The connection of this song with *farce double* lies, I was told, in an analogy between the stars and the holes in the lid of the roasting pit" (*Stories*, 31). Yet later, describing the annual "feast of *farce double*," the narrator suggests several other connections: the feast is a time "for enemies to forgive one another;" at its origin it was associated with second marriages ("some writers think this gave the dish its name"); because it coincides with the arrival of the shepherds with their flocks, it makes concrete the connections between "the settled mountain craftsmen" and "the semi-nomadic shepherds" and reminds one that "marriages between them have been recorded since the founding of the village. . . . Perhaps the legend of second marriages reflects a practice whereby a widow or widower took a spouse among the folk of which he was not a member" (*Stories*, 35–36). In the song about the young man, his father has remarried, and his stepmother "does for him what mother never did for her son"; his leaving home causes a breach that is healed when he returns; he is a blacksmith, his love a shepherdess. Is the narrator ignorant or is he or she being ironic in calling attention to a most tenuous connection between the story and *farce double* and ignoring the much more obvious connections? And does the dwelling upon the connection between *farce double* and second marriages suggest something about the narrator? Thus "Country Cooking" contains not one but several stories within an outrageous recipe. And it leaves yet another story to be made up by the reader.

"The Novel as History" presents the reader with an even more enigmatic narrator—or I should say, two narrators. Most of this story is related by an old man named Robinson. We are told in the first sentence that he "was seated in front of the fire" and in the last sentence that he "irritably . . . poked the lowering coals." Between these two sentences Robinson is the sole speaker. All we know about the person to whom he is speaking is that he has mentioned Robinson's "encounter with Rouxinol" (*Stories*, 52). At the end Robinson tells him, "Keep watching [the bridge in the valley below]—the lights should go on any moment now" (*Stories*, 58).

Robinson's monologue begins, "I knew Johns. . . . I met him in Detroit in '38." Johns was saved from death by Rouxinol who in turn was saved by "Borgmann, the Danish lepidopterist" who "was travelling with old Jeremiah Keats" who persuaded "Ketchum . . . to leave England and come to Chile" where he "met Bechstein, the 'nurse at Waterloo' of the historical classic of that name" (*Stories*, 52–53). Robinson continues, ranging, in seven pages, over 31 people (with several asides) while ranging in space around the world and in time from the present to the Middle Ages and back to the present once again. The links in the chain seem to be connected only by Robinson's memory until he comes to Nicholas Scriptor, a medieval clerk, and his sister "Anne, abbess of the great Yorkshire convent of Poor Clares. Abbess Anne was a Stonebottle, the first known to us of the line that so brilliantly carried out the injunction of the family arms, *Floreat colus* ('Let the distaff flourish')" (*Stories*, 57). He then traces the Stonebottle women (in two paragraphs) from medieval England to America where Catharine helped Betsy Ross with the flag, and Patricia accompanied Lewis and Clark on their expedition. Christina revolutionized battlefield surgery during the First World War. And Jane "erected the Elizabeth Palmer Peabody Bridge that is to be inaugurated this evening in the valley below us" (*Stories*, 58).

The title ("The Novel as History") suggests a connection between the inauguration of the bridge and Robinson's irritation in the final sentence, but the reader is never given the connection, and we are left wondering if the person to whom Robinson is speaking (whoever he or she is) has come because of the inauguration or if the visit is a coincidence or an accident (to use the distinction made in "The Dialect of the Tribe"). One can well imagine this narrative occurring, without change, in *The Conversions*, where the context might give it meaning or render it absurd. But perhaps Mathews's point is that the reader needs but the barest suggestion to create his story, to turn history into fiction—or (like Robinson?) to turn fiction into history.

"Tradition and the Individual Talent: The 'Bratislava Spiccato'" is somewhat similar to "The Novel as History" in its use of numerous family and social relationships: "This was the Jenö Szenkar whose wife's elder brother was the grandfather of Geza Anda. Benno Bennewitz for his part was Teresa Stich-Randall's maternal great-grandfather, and his niece was Dietrich Fischer-Dieskau's mother. . . . [Szenkar] had become involved in bitter public controversy with Ludwig Krumpholz (who, much later, was Hermann Scherchen's godfather) over the performance of the cadenzas in Joseph-Leopold Pitsch's posthumous piano concerto. Pitsch's widow, the following year, was to marry Karl Knappertsbusch and by him bear the father of Hans Knappertsbusch" (*Stories*, 82–83).

We are told that Szenkar's helper Franz Mittag "as an infant had shared a wetnurse with Irmgaard Dehn, for whom her granddaughter Irmgaard Seefried was named" and that Mittag "was named only two years later to the directorship of the opera, after a year's interim under the aging Julius Meyer-Remy, the great-grandfather of both Hugo Meyer-Welfing and Mrs. Rudolph Bing." Szenkar has a stroke and dies "during a rehearsal of *Childe Harold*. This now-forgotten opera was by Bela Hubay, whose great-grandson married George Szell's sister" (*Stories*, 83–84). None of these people—Anda, Stich-Randall, Fischer-Dieskau, Scherchen, Pitsch's widow, Karl and Hans Knappertsbusch, Dehn, Seefried, Meyer-Remy, Meyer-Welfing, Bing, Hubay, George Szell's sister—have anything to do with the "story." For "Tradition and the Individual Talent" differs from "The Novel as History" in at least two important ways: it does contain something of a story, and it is related by a detached narrator.

The story is a simple one: the conductor Szenkar becomes involved with Krumpholz in an argument over the performance of the cadenzas in Pitsch's concerto. He goes to Graz to visit with his old friend Bennewitz and recuperate from the strain of the controversy, but he dies in Budapest a week after leaving Graz. Czegka, a violinist and lifelong friend of Szenkar, plans to attend the memorial ceremony for him in Budapest. During the train journey he completes a line of thought begun when he attended the performance of the controversial Pitsch concerto, during which the pianist Krumpholz had produced a "novel effect, that of making the hammers 'bounce drily' on the strings" (*Stories*, 86). Czegka has been trying to discover a way to make a violin bow produce a similar effect. As the train arrives at the Bratislava station, Czegka makes his discovery. His excitement produces a heart attack, he stumbles on the platform, and, just before he dies, whispers his discovery to a Russian Rabbi. The Rabbi repeats it to Zaremba of the St. Petersburg Conservatory. "These facts," the narrator concludes, "supply a partial explanation of the excellence of Russian violinists in the twentieth century, and clarify the origins of the controversial expression "Bratislava spiccato'" (*Stories*, 88).

The dizzying digressions into irrelevant family and social relationships that distract the reader from the main line of the narrative are not justified, as perhaps they are in "The Novel as History," by a garrulous old

narrator. Instead, we seem to have what is rare in Mathews's fiction, a
detached, omniscient narrator—in this instance a music critic. But the
title, taken from one of T. S. Eliot's most famous essays, indicates that
we are not to equate the speaker with Mathews. Eliot wrestles with one
of the thorniest problems in literature: the relationship between the
writer and his age. His conclusion is that the age—and through it the
tradition that produced the age—is of crucial importance to the development of individual genius. And though he is vague as to the nature of
the relationship, he insists that there *is* one tradition that ultimately
causes that development. It is possible to read Mathews's story in just
the opposite way, as suggesting that the discovery of the "Bratislava
Spiccato" was merely one of countless possibilities. Or that the discovery,
for all the appearance of a dependence upon an intricate web of relationships, ultimately depended for its effect upon a pure coincidence. Or was
it a coincidence that the Russian Rabbi happened to be in the railway
station? After all, we are not told *his* story but only that, luckily, he
knew German and that he "was Nathan Milstein's father" (*Stories*, 87). Is
the narrator being ironic? Is he satirizing the notion that there is any
cause-and-effect relationship between tradition and individual talent?
Or is Mathews making use of dramatic irony? Do we, the readers, realize something the narrator does not? Though "Tradition and the
Individual Talent" has a more fully developed narrative than "The Novel
as History," we are nonetheless given a story that forces us to create our
own story. And this effect is once again accomplished through a subtle
manipulation of point of view.

## Literature as Play

Mathews's short fiction puts into action his idea of literature as play;
that idea is most forcefully expressed as theory in an address delivered in
1982 ("Prizewinners," 7–20). Dismissing the older notion that in fiction
writer and reader participate through "communication," Mathews offers
a "new conception" of the relationship between reader and writer. In so
doing he reverses two basic tenets of Realism: (1) it is not the writer but
the reader who is the creator; (2) the writer chooses "a terrain unfamiliar
to both the reader and himself" ("Prizewinners," 9). The first of these
ideas, the opposite of Wolfe's idea of the writer as "reporter," has already
been discussed. When Mathews says, "The writer must take care to do
no more than supply the reader with the materials and (as we often say
nowadays) the space to create an experience" ("Prizewinners," 10), we

should note that Mathews doesn't mean what the Imagists meant, that the author recreates (imitates) nature in such a way that the reader reacts to it in the same way that the author reacted, that the imagination causes us to eliminate overt moralizing from art and replace it with a more subtle moral vision grounded in sensation. Mathews means something much more radical: "writing works exclusively by what the writer leaves out. . . . The nothingness the writer offers the reader opens up space—a space that acknowledges that the reader, not the writer, is the sole creator" ("Prizewinners," 13).

Mathews's second point, that the writer chooses "a terrain unfamiliar to both the reader and himself," is, as he says, "harder to explain." At first glance it would seem he is the kind of writer that Wolfe attacks, but he goes on to say that "the unfamiliar matter the writer chooses is nothing else than his own story" ("Prizewinners," 10). To explain how "one's own story" can be "unfamiliar" to that person Mathews makes a psychological distinction between our *conscious* image of ourselves (the stories we generate from that image for both others and ourselves) and our "real stories," which, according to Proust, lie hidden within us and have to be "decoded." He cites Proust's comparison of "the writer's task of translating the symbols within him to the deciphering of hieroglyphs" ("Prizewinners," 10). We shouldn't be surprised, considering his novels and short fiction, to find Mathews talking of the creative process in terms of codes and hieroglyphs. And when he attempts to explain how the writer gets to the hidden inner self, his explanation becomes something of a cipher. He cites three entrances to the inner self: personal history, the body, and consciousness. Characteristically, he reverses the first and says that the act of writing opens up memory rather than the other way around (thus games, puzzles, and constraints). The next two, body and consciousness, seem to be substitutes for the more traditional "imagery" and "imagination."

Writing must make a sensual appeal, so writing must in part come from the physical, the body. To accomplish this "writers should make a point of keeping what they write in touch with how they speak. . . . What you have to write down may strike you as chaotic, vulgar, and undignified. This makes no difference—you can clean it up later." Finally:

> By consciousness I do not mean your feelings, or your ideas, or your imagination; I mean what you feel *with*, what you have ideas *with*, what you imagine *with*. Not the voice chattering in the back of your head

telling you what's right and wrong, rather what enables you to hear that
voice, and also what enables you to hear yourself listening to that voice.
Not your experience: your awareness of experience. . . . [W]e might say
that consciousness generates not meaning but the power to create meaning. It does not produce a particular meaning—it produces no conclusions. Instead, it has the capacity of creating meaning again and again,
one meaning after another. We could also describe it as an infinite poten-
tiality of meaning. ("Prizewinners," 11–12)

Mathews seems to be describing a spiritual dimension in human
nature, what others would call a soul, which has the power to "create."
Mathews's analogy, "the star-filled sky," at first appears to suggest something other than the soul. Throughout the ages, according to Mathews,

the night sky has been looked on as a vision that must be deciphered. . . .
While interpretations of the sky have changed many times and are still
changing, what has not changed is this desire to understand. . . .
Whatever formulations the long process of explanation may have yielded
strike me as not mattering much when they are confronted with the overwhelming desire for knowledge that the night sky never fails to inspire.
This desire is expressed as speculation—a word that etymologically signifies mirroring. What the night sky mirrors is ourselves, and it will serve
as a mirror of what I have called our consciousness. ("Prizewinners,"
12–13)

The shift from "understanding" to "knowledge" to "speculation" is
difficult to follow, but once again it's not surprising to find Mathews
talking of meaning in terms of "deciphering" and "speculation," leading
one to think that he limits this capacity in man to the faculty of reason,
to a desire, he says, "to know everything." But when he goes on to say
that "the consciousness is capable . . . of knowing not only anything but
everything," he moves beyond reason to an act of faith, which he then
dissolves in an insistence on nothingness as the source of meaning:
"[Writers] must provide nothings. . . . They make the experience of consciousness available through nothings—absences, negations, voids. To
put it another way, writing works exclusively by what the writer leaves
out" ("Prizewinners," 13).

Mathews illustrates his point with the opening of Jane Austen's
*Northanger Abbey*, asserting, "With one exception . . . what we learn
about Catherine is all the things she isn't," which means that "we, the
readers, are invited to think up what she is" ("Prize-winners," 13). The

one exception is a description of Catherine at age 10 that makes her out to be very plain, even unattractive, which, according to Mathews, "is the last thing we want to hear." But then we are told that at 15 "appearances were mending," and she is becoming *"almost* pretty," a fact that pleases Catherine because, like the reader, she had not liked her unattractiveness. "Catherine feels exactly the way we do. The fact of her plainness has been sticking in her craw, and when that plainness goes she experiences a relief like our own. For a moment, without warning, and of course *without* being told, we become Catherine. She and I are briefly the same person. As a result, I am propelled head- and heartlong into her story" ("Prizewinners," 15).

So according to Mathews, "[T]he first step a writer takes to ensure participation in the domain of consciousness is to supply the reader with negations and absences. . . . The writer provides a void, the reader fills it up . . . but you should realize that such movement or action bears no resemblance to narrative action" ("Prizewinners," 14). Mathews must be speaking—to a certain extent—metaphorically since the words provided by the author do not literally constitute a void. And Mathews's choice of example, a novel that is primarily a satire, a parody, raises some questions since Austen is counting on her readers to be familiar with the works she is satirizing.

In his next example, a passage from Kafka, Mathews attempts to prove what Joyce and somewhat later Pound asserted, that rhythm is central in fiction, that there is a rhythm for every emotion. He twice rewrites Kafka's fable drawn from *Don Quixote* to illustrate that the "syntax" (by which he means a combination of style, rhythm, and structure) is more important than the "content." But since his substitutions never remove the reference to *Don Quixote*, it is debatable as to whether or not his rewriting really proves anything.

But Mathews is an artist, and the logic and consistency of his critical stance are not as important as his insistence upon the importance of the reader to the development of great literature. His examples from Kafka and Austen, along with his idea that the writer must deal with what he is most unfamiliar with, that is, his own life, all come together in his idea of fiction as play. The writer provides playing field and rules (the unfamiliar, constraints) for himself and out of them he shapes the playing field for the reader. Within the bounds of the playing field—absences and negations—the reader creates whatever "reality" the work has.

What is central here is the word "creates." If a work of fiction is a game, then the reader participates in such a way as to determine its outcome, just as an individual or a team involved in a sport determines its outcome, who wins or loses. For a work of fiction to be truly a game, the reader must be in control since the significance of a game lies within the game itself. Metaphor, as we saw in chapter 1, holds a somewhat ambiguous position in twentieth-century fiction since on the one hand it unifies but on the other hand it unifies in relation to something outside the work. The question would seem to be, can one have unity without "meaning"? and the answer would seem to be, "yes, if 'meaning' is purely relative." Which 'means,' of course, that meaning cannot be "communicated"—thus Mathews's rejection of direct writer-to-reader communication as a basic principle of fiction ("Prizewinners," 9).

The notion of a novel as a tennis court will doubtless seem strange to many people—not only to those who look for morals or messages in literature but also to those who look for a communal emotional significance, a shared experience that extends beyond the relationship between writer and reader. It's one thing to assert that literature grows out of and expresses a culture, and when that culture fades, the literature takes on whatever meaning the new culture assigns it; it's quite another to assert that any work of literature is the ad hoc creation of its readers, one by one, from the day it is published. Such a view is the exact opposite of that of Wolfe and the Realists, who think the writer should present the reader with a report of a game that has already been played. But both sides would agree on one point: fiction cannot *be* life. Thus the Realists would make it a substitute for life, while Mathews and the Oulipians would make it a part of the *play* they call life.

For Mathews, then, the only absolute truth would seem to be the search for truth: "While the 'desire for meaning' is absolute, meanings themselves 'never are final'; indeed, 'if there is an ultimate meaning,' Mathews argues, 'it will be nothing'" (McPheron, 198). If there is nothing beyond the outer darkness, nothing out there to "discover" but nothing itself, then the fullness of life resides in the doing more than in the done. The old Aristotelian/Thomist view of art was that its value resides in that which is made and not in the maker, a view that caused Wilde to assert that for a man to be a poisoner is nothing against his prose. In Mathews's view, since the creator is the reader, one would have to say that the reader's being a poisoner has much to do with the reality the reader creates, which is, as far as the reader is concerned, the work of art.

The middle ground between Realism and play is ritual. Kenneth Koch observes: "Claude Levi-Strauss said the difference between a ritual and a game was that a ritual was a game that always turned out the

same way. Harry Mathews's novels have in them something of both."[6]
He then cites "very strict standards . . . the rigor and arbitrariness of ceremony" as evidence of ritual in Mathews's work, while the novels' game-
like quality is evident in that they are "totally unpredictable."

Ritual is a term usually associated in literature with tragedy, which
seeks to make the audience participants in the action not as the players
in a game who determine the outcome but as members of a community
who experience the old rhythms of existence: birth, joy, suffering, death.
Modernism, in using the relativism of science as a unifying principle, can
be seen as the supreme attempt to make fiction find itself through ritual.
This observation brings us full circle back to where we started: relativism
could be unified only by an appeal to an absolute. Not that the society
has to know what the absolute consists of but only that it exists. Such a
belief is called faith, and what Wolfe and the social realists fail to indicate
is that the faith of the writers before the twentieth century was different
from that of the writers who followed. The Victorian novelist believed in
order and sought to discover it; the modernist sought to represent the
fragmentation of life in relation to an unknowable transcendent reality.

In other words, what lay at the heart of modernist fiction was mystery. And mystery is central to the work of Mathews as well. In each of
the novels there are mysteries—enigmas—that remain unsolved. Each
player (reader) must come up with his or her own solutions. But each
novel also turns on a deeper mystery: the relationship of the narrator (or
narrators) to the action. When Koch says that Mathews's novels are
unpredictable, he is referring to plot, to narrative. But if one believes
that the highest truth is that we continue to search for truth, that all our
endeavors end in speculation, then Mathews's plots—his many "stories"—are part of a ritual, the endless acting out by each individual of
the search for truth. And being rituals, the "endings" are predictable: the
narrator of *The Conversions* begins "paying his debts," the narrator of
*Tlooth* vanishes into a print hanging from her wall, Twang sends a letter
that may or may not reach its destination, Lewis comes to believe that
every search becomes a part of the next search, that each of us "carries
the accumulated weight of the generations succeeding one another."
What is predictable is that there are countless endings but no End.

So Mathews closes his address to students with the following advice:
"Choose your subjects the way you used to choose your toys: out of
desire. You have the universe for your toy shop now. The time has come
for you to go out and play" ("Prizewinners," 20). For many such a view

of existence will seem frivolous. But in a universe devoid of absolutes, play is the highest seriousness. Others will ask why it is that we "have the universe" at all, and when they come to the end of *Cigarettes* where the narrator calls attention to "the immortal presence of that original and heroic actor who saw that the world had been given him to play in without remorse or fear," they will ask, "Given him by whom?" Such readers will find Mathews a modernist. For them his games will become a part of that ancient ritual, the search for truth, that governs the life and art of all who believe existence to be a mystery never entirely solved by accurate reporting or by the manipulation of words on a page.

# Notes and References

*Chapter One*

1. Harry Mathews, *The Way Home: Collected Longer Prose* (London: Atlas Press, 1989), 160; hereafter cited in text as *Way Home*.

2. Lynne Tillman, "Harry Mathews," *Bomb*, no. 26 (Winter 1988–89): 34; an interview; hereafter cited in text.

3. William McPherson, "Harry Mathews: A Checklist," *Review of Contemporary Fiction* 7, no. 3 (Fall 1987): 197–226; hereafter cited in text; includes an excellent introduction summarizing the reaction to Mathews's fiction on both sides of the Atlantic.

4. Harry Mathews, interview with author, 1989. See chapter 2; hereafter cited in text as Interview.

5. John Ash, "A Conversation with Harry Mathews," *Review of Contemporary Fiction* 7, no. 3 (Fall 1987): 26; hereafter cited in text.

6. The intricacies of the New Criticism, and in particular its own paradoxical debt to Coleridge and the romantics (paradoxical because a tenet of the New Criticism was a rejection of romanticism), have been endlessly analyzed, attacked, and defended. I am interested here only in its central insistence on meaning. The other major critical stances—formalism and archetypal interpretation—respectively, rejected transcendent meaning and imposed it from without.

7. E. M. Forster, *Aspects of the Novel* (New York: Harcourt, Brace, 1927), 130–31.

8. Hugh Kenner, *Ulysses* (London: George Allen & Unwin, 1980), 61–71.

9. John Ashbery, "John Ashbery Interviewing Harry Mathews," *Review of Contemporary Fiction* 7, no. 3 (Fall 1987): 41; hereafter cited in text.

10. Raymond Roussel, *How I Wrote Certain of My Books* (New York: Sun, 1977). See also Rayner Heppenstall, *Raymond Roussel* (Berkeley: University of California Press, 1967).

11. Alain Robbe-Grillet, *For a New Novel* (New York: Grove Press, 1965), 79–80; hereafter cited in text.

12. For example, John Ashbery's two essays in *How I Wrote Certain of My Books* (see note 10) and Michel Foucault's *Death and the Labyrinth* (Garden City, N.Y.: Doubleday, 1986).

13. Linda Hutcheon, *Narcissistic Narrative* (Waterloo, Ontario: Wilfrid Laurier University Press, 1980), 36–47.

14. Oscar Wilde, "The Devoted Friend," in *Novels and Fairy Tales of Oscar Wilde* (New York: Cosmopolitan Book Corp., 1915), 677–93; hereafter cited in text.

15.   A statement made by Wilde in many forms in many different places. This one is taken from "The Truth of Masks," quoted in Richard Ellmann, *Oscar Wilde* (New York: Knopf, 1988), 99.

16.   The notable exceptions are "The Portrait of Mr. W. H." and "The Sphinx without a Secret."

*Chapter Two*

1.   Evelyn Waugh, "Ronald Firbank," in *Ronald Firbank: Memoirs and Critiques* (London: Duckworth, 1977), 175–79. First published in *Life & Letters*, July 1929.

2.   Keith Cohen, "The Labors of the Signifier," *Review of Contemporary Fiction* 7, no. 3 (Fall 1987): 173.

*Chapter Three*

1.   Harry Mathews, *The Conversions*, in *The Sinking of the Odradek Stadium and Other Novels* (New York: Harper & Row, 1975), 3; hereafter cited in text as *Conversions*.

2.   Should Mathews become famous, critics and scholars will make careers tracing these patterns. Already an excellent model is provided by Tomasz Mirkowicz's study of the mythological allusions and themes in "Harry Mathews's *The Conversions*: In the Net of the Goddess," *Review of Contemporary Fiction* 7, no. 3 (Fall 1987): 100–109.

3.   Then again, maybe he does, since "the Old Man's Beard," along with metaphysical dentistry, turns up in *Tlooth*, just as Evelyn Roak turns up in *The Sinking of the Odradek Stadium* and just as (I'll bet) something or someone from *Odradek* probably turns up in *Cigarettes*.

*Chapter Four*

1.   Harry Mathews, *Tlooth*, in *The Sinking of the Odradek Stadium and Other Novels* (New York: Harper & Row, 1975), 188–89; hereafter cited in text as *Tlooth*.

2.   At least I hope so since one of the main prisons in Georgia, U.S.A., is in the town of Jackson.

3.   Ash finds a similarity with the opening of Firbank's *Vainglory*, and Mathews agrees. I don't see it except that both Mathews and Firbank surprise the ear and, as Mathews remarks, make their openings a little difficult for the reader. See Ash, 21.

4.   William McPheron bases this conclusion on a study of "interviews and other statements of self-characterization" and on "the tapes of Mathews's very informative 13–16 November 1983 residency at the 80 Langston Street gallery in San Francisco."

5.   Eric Mottram believes the narrator to be "androgenous" and "bisexually married to another called Joan." He begins by referring to the narrator as "he" and changes to "he/she" and "his/her." Eric Mottram, "'Eleusions Truths': Harry Mathews's Strategies and Games," *Review of Contemporary Fiction* 7, no. 3 (Fall 1987): 157; hereafter cited in text.

## Chapter Five

1.   Harry Mathews, *The Sinking of the Odradek Stadium and Other Novels* (New York: Harper & Row, 1975), 365; hereafter cited in text as *Odradek*.

2.   It should be noted, however, that the "editor" does let some errors stand uncorrected. For example, "I hittd him" (*Odradek*, 540) and "thck as a chocolate brownie" (*Odradek*, 541).

3.   For example, Joseph McElroy, "Harry Mathews's Fiction: A Map of Masks," *Review of Contemporary Fiction* 7, no. 3 (Fall 1987): 85.

4.   This may be playfulness on Mathews's part since I have not been able to find this phrase in any of the standard dictionaries of slang (though of course *blow* and *chase* are common enough).

5.   Flann O'Brien, *At Swim-Two-Birds* (London: Four Square Books, 1962), 5.

6.   Georges Perec, *Life A User's Manual* (Boston: David R. Godine, 1987), {xiv–xv]; hereafter cited in text.

7.   Peter Hutchinson, *Games Authors Play* (New York: Methuen, 1983), 11–12ff. Hutchinson uses the terms to describe the relationships between writer and reader in literary game playing.

## Chapter Six

1.   Edmund White, "Their Masks, Their Lives—Harry Mathews's *Cigarettes*," *Review of Contemporary Fiction* 7, no. 3 (Fall 1987): 77.

2.   We are told, "If the painting looked inspired, what else did it look like? Certainly not Elizabeth." And "the gold and white of the face . . . the ocher of the eyes . . . the mauve lips" are alluded to (Harry Mathews, *Cigarettes* [New York: Weidenfeld & Nicolson, 1987], 157); hereafter cited in text as *Cigarettes*.

3.   The longest reference to the war comes in a one-paragraph aside on page 231 where we learn that during the war, probably in 1942, Allan served in the Pacific, and Maude briefly took a lover.

4.   Actually, Mathews seems to give two different dates. He states that Priscilla was 14 years old (241) and that Lewis was 15 (177), which would make it the summer of 1954; but elsewhere he says that it occurred in the summer of 1956 ("Six years before [1962, i.e., 1956], they had had a serious falling out" [161].

5.   Harry Mathews, *Twenty Lines a Day* (Elmwood Park, Ill.: Dalky Archive Press, 1988), 84.

6.   Harry Mathews, "For Prizewinners," *Review of Contemporary Fiction* 7, no. 3 (Fall 1987): 10; hereafter cited in text as "Prizewinners."

7.   William McPheron makes the following observation: "The contrast between American tension and French ease [in dealing with such works as Mathews's 'Singular Pleasures'] is striking and recalls Mathews's earlier observation that 'I have less of a problem in getting immediate acceptance from French readers but ultimately I think only Americans could understand what I'm doing' because his writing is 'essentially . . . very American' (*Silo* interview, 1978)." See McPheron, 201.

*Chapter Seven*

1.   Tom Wolfe, "Stalking the Billion-Footed Beast," *Harper's*, Nov. 1989, 45–56; hereafter cited in text.

2.   See "Letters" in the February and March 1990 issues of *Harper's*.

3.   W. W. Canning, "Remarks on the Character and Writing of John Milton," quoted in Richard Weaver, *The Ethics of Rhetoric* (Davis, Calif.: Hermagoras Press, 1985), 143.

4.   Harry Mathews, *Country Cooking and Other Stories* (Providence, R.I.: Burning Deck, 1980), 59–62; hereafter cited in text as *Stories*.

5.   In *Selected Declarations of Dependence*, Mathews limits himself to words contained in 44 proverbs.

6.   Kenneth Koch, "About Harry Mathews's Fiction," *Review of Contemporary Fiction* 7, no. 3 (Fall 1987): 110.

# Selected Bibliography

PRIMARY SOURCES

*Novels*

*Cigarettes*. New York: Weidenfeld & Nicolson, 1987.
*The Conversions*. New York: Random House, 1962.
*The Sinking of the Odradek Stadium and Other Novels*. New York: Harper & Row, 1975. Includes reprints of *The Conversions* and *Tlooth*.
*Tlooth*. Garden City, N.Y.: Doubleday/Paris Review Editions, 1966.

*Other Fiction and Poetry*

*The American Experience*. London: Atlas Press, 1991
*Armenian Papers: Poems 1954–84*. Princeton: Princeton University Press, 1987.
*Country Cooking and Other Stories*. Providence, R.I.: Burning Deck, 1980.
*A Mid-Season Sky: Poems 1954–1991*. Manchester: Carcanet, 1992.
*Out of Bounds*. Providence, R.I.: Burning Deck Chapbook Series, 1989.
*The Planisphere*. Providence, R.I.: Burning Deck, 1974.
*The Ring: Poems 1956–69*. Leeds, England: Juillard Editions, 1970.
*Selected Declarations of Dependence*. Calais, Vt.: Z Press, 1977.
*Trial Impressions*. Providence, R.I.: Burning Deck, 1977.
*The Way Home: Collected Longer Prose*. London: Atlas Press, 1989. Contains "The Orchard" (1988) and "Singular Pleasures" (1988), and an autobiographical essay from the Gale Contemporary Authors: Autobiographical Series (1988).

*Nonfiction*

*Immeasurable Distances: The Collected Essays*. Venice, CA.: The Lapic Press, 1991.
*20 Lines a Day*. Elmwood Park, Ill.: Dalkey Archive Press, 1988.
"We for One: An Introduction to Joseph McElroy's *Men and Women*," *Review of Contemporary Fiction* 10, no. 1 (Spring 1990): 199–226.

*Translations*

Bataille, George. *Blue of Noon* (*Le Bleu du Ciel*). New York: Urizen, 1978.
Chaix, Marie. *The Laurels of Lake Constance* (*Les Lauriers du Lac de Constance*). New York: Viking, 1977.
Cordelier, Jeanne. *The Life* (*La Dérobade*). New York: Viking, 1978.

## SECONDARY SOURCES

Ehrmann, Jacques. *Game, Play, Literature*. Boston: Beacon Press, 1968. Early outline of play theory as it applies to literature.

Foucault, Michel. *Death and the Labyrinth*. Garden City, N.Y.: Doubleday, 1986. Controversial study of Roussel.

Graves, Robert. *The White Goddess*. New York: Farrar, Straus and Giroux, 1966. For those interested in the background of *The Conversions*.

Horder, Mervyn. *Ronald Firbank: Memoirs and Critiques*. London: Duckworth, 1977. Good introduction to Firbank.

Kostelanetz, Richard, ed. *The Avant-Garde Tradition in Literature*. Buffalo, N.Y.: Prometheus Books, 1982. Contains a review by Mathews of Perec's *La Disparition*.

McCaffrey, Larry, ed. *Postmodern Fiction: A Bio-Bibliographical Guide*. New York: Greenwood Press, 1986. Contains essay on Mathews by Welch D. Everman.

Maurer, David W. *Language of the Underworld*. Lexington, Ky.: University of Kentucky Press, 1981. Handy reference for deciphering argot of confidence men.

Mercier, Vivian. *The New Novel: From Queneau to Pinget*. New York: Farrar, Straus & Giroux, 1971. Workmanlike introduction to French New Novelists.

Moore, Steven. *William Gaddis*. Boston: Twayne, 1989. Excellent study of the writer who has exerted a major influence on much postwar American fiction.

Motte, Warren F., Jr. *Oulipo: A Primer of Potential Literature*. Lincoln, Neb.: University of Nebraska Press, 1986. Essay on the organization, as well as a poem and essay by Mathews and works by other members.

Perec, Georges. *Life A User's Manual*. Boston: David R. Godine, 1987. Preamble contains jigsaw puzzle metaphor.

*Review of Contemporary Fiction* 7, no. 3 (Fall 1987). Indispensable edition focusing on Harry Mathews. Contains two interviews, 16 essays, and an excellent bibliography of work by and on Mathews through 1987.

Robbe-Grillet, Alain. *For a New Novel*. Translated by Richard Howard. New York: Grove Press, 1965. Contains the dominant avant-garde French view of fiction in the 1950s.

Roussel, Raymond. *How I Wrote Certain of My Books*. Translated by Trevor Winkfield. New York: Sun, 1977. Roussel's explanation of some of his self-imposed constraints.

Sacks, Sheldon, ed. *On Metaphor*. Chicago: University of Chicago Press, 1979.

Stonehill, Brian. "On Harry Mathews," *Chicago Review* 33, no. 2 (1982): 107–11. Intelligent general essay.

Tillman, Lynne. "Harry Mathews," *Bomb* no. 26 (Winter 1988–89): 34–37. Interview.

# Index

# The Author

Warren Leamon, a native of Atlanta, Georgia, attended Davidson College, the University of Georgia, Vanderbilt University, and University College, Dublin, Ireland (Ph.D. 1974). He has published essays on Anglo-Irish, English, and American literature in quarterlies and journals in the United States, Canada, and Ireland. He has also published poetry and fiction as well as a novel, *Unheard Melodies* (Longstreet Press, 1990). He has served as poetry and fiction editor of the Georgia Review. Currently, he lives in Japan where he teaches modern English and American literature at Hiroshima University.

## The Editor

Frank Day is a professor of English at Clemson University. He is the author of Sir William Empson: An Annotated Bibliography and Arthur Koestler: A Guide to Research. He was a Fulbright Lecturer in American Literature in Romania (1980–81) and in Bangladesh (1986–87).